Design in mind

Design in mind

Bryan Lawson

Butterworth Architecture
An imprint of Butterworth-Heinemann Ltd
Linacre House, Jordan Hill, Oxford OX2 8DP

ℛ A member of the Reed Elsevier group

OXFORD LONDON BOSTON
MUNICH NEW DELHI SINGAPORE SYDNEY
TOKYO TORONTO WELLINGTON

First published 1994

British Library Cataloguing in Publication Data
Lawson, Bryan
Design in mind
I. Title
721

Library of Congress Cataloging-in-Publication Data
Lawson, Bryan
Design in mind/Bryan Lawson
p. cm.
Includes bibliographical references and index.
ISBN 0 7506 1211 8
1. Architectural design   I. Title
NA2750.L38   93–50198
720–dc20   CIP

Cover illustrations: proposals for Temasek Polytechnic in Singapore by Michael Wilford
and Partners, and Cathedral of St. John The Divine in New York by Santiago Calatrava.

Typeset by TecSet Ltd, Wallington, Surrey
Printed in Great Britain

Contents

Acknowledgements

I am, of course, extremely grateful to all the designers whose work is reviewed in this book. They have all given of their precious time very generously, but, more importantly, have entered into the spirit of this enquiry in such a manner as to make the task of compiling this book a fascinating and thoroughly rewarding experience. I consider it a great privilege to be allowed so close to the workings of so many fine designers.

In addition to the named principals of the practices studied, I was given considerable help by many other members of staff in their offices. Their names would form a formidable list so I hope they will forgive me for not including them all.

Thanks are due to many colleagues and students who have helped to clarify and develop arguments. However, particular thanks go to Mohammed Abu Bakar who, in the early phases of this project, assisted so much with a great deal of the research which was to inform the interviews.

The conversations which I had with the designers in this book were often animated and frequently relied heavily on drawings and gestures as well as words. Transcribing such discussions from tapes is therefore a somewhat unenviable task and thanks are due to Joanne Clarkson for completing it with such patience.

Bryan Lawson

Introduction

The great majority of books on design offer criticism and analysis of the end products of the design process whether they be in the form of products, interiors, buildings, landscape or urban areas. By contrast, this book deals with the process itself rather than the end product, and is thus concerned with that most magical and precious of all human activity – the creation of something new and original. The author has studied both architecture and psychology and continues to be fascinated by the possibility of understanding the design process through scientific investigations. Perhaps one of the reasons for this fascination lies in the contrasting nature of knowledge in science and design. The scientific process is made explicit and replicable, while designers rarely reveal or discuss their methods. Papers in scientific journals are scrutinized not only for the correctness of method but also for the accuracy of description of that method. A design, on the other hand, will only appear in a journal or magazine if it is seen to have merit in itself. Scientists do a job that is essentially one of description, that is, they try to tell us how things are. Designers, on the other hand, are prescriptive since their job is to tell us how things ought to be. We expect design to have artistic values, and yet design is also more than art, for designs must not only express appropriate ideas and values but must also be usable and work.

Design as a professional activity separated from the making of things is a relatively recent phenomenon, and the investigation of design is still in its infancy. In the early years of serious design research it became fashionable to see design as an entirely generic and field-independent activity. Thus a respected worker in the field, Sydney Gregory, could confidently assert that 'the process of design is the same whether it deals with the design of a new oil refinery, the construction of a cathedral or the writing of Dante's *Divine Comedy*' (Gregory, 1966). The author of this book is not entirely convinced of this view and rather doubts that Dante would be either! However, in everyday language 'design' refers to an enormous range of activities from the highly constrained, numerical, and well-defined problems of, say, electronic engineering to the underconstrained, nebulous and ill-defined problems in, say, fashion and textiles (Lawson, 1990).

This book in concerned with architectural design, but the issues raised may well be seen as generic enough to apply to other similar design fields, which would include industrial and product design, interior design, urban design and at least some areas of structural engineering. These fields all share in common a three-dimensional end product which will be lived in or used directly by people who are likely to be concerned about both its appearance and physical performance. These fields are now generally recognized as presenting 'wicked' problems (Rittel and Webber, 1973). By this is meant that these problems defy complete description and lack the clarity of formulation found in scientific problems. They are the sort of problems where the information you need to understand them rather depends upon your ideas for solving them. This sort of design then is a 'knowledge-rich' as opposed to 'knowledge-lean' activity. In other words, design requires us to have considerable amounts of knowledge beyond that which is stated in the problem description. Above all, we must recognize that design is a process in which there will be no one recognizably correct or even optimal answer. These are the defining characteristics of the design fields studied here. The reader must judge the extent to which these ideas are capable of application in other design fields.

The great philosopher Ludwig Wittgenstein is reported to have said 'you think philosophy is difficult enough, but I tell you it is nothing to the difficulty of being a good architect'. Architecture represents a particularly challenging form of design, lying as it does near the middle of the spectrum of activity about which we use the word 'design'. Today architecture is in a state of some confusion. There is no clear school of thought as there was during the Modern Movement and certainly no consensus about style as there was in earlier periods. In a sense this is very exciting because since little can be taken for granted we are constantly challenged to develop a clearer view about design as an end product and consequently also about design as a process.

If we want to understand the design process there are several types of technique we can employ. We can analyse the task and propose logical structures and processes that we imagine must or should take place. We can observe designers at work. We can conduct laboratory experiments on designers. Finally, we can ask designers to tell us what they do.

The early years of design methods research were characterized by the first approach. Many have proposed design methods based on what they think should happen rather than based on any evidence that it actually does. Such work was easily criticized and often dismissed by practising designers as irrelevant and unrealistic, but actually it provided an invaluable contribution towards defining the subject and mapping out some of the questions to which we wanted answers.

Observing designers at work has never been a popular technique, since their external behaviour is not particularly revealing about their mental processes. The drawings which designers produce as they work are often specifically to examine particular issues, and may appear quite incomprehensible to an objective observer. Some investigators, including this author, have conducted experiments on designers, but these are notoriously difficult to devise and control without resorting to highly artificial laboratory situations.

Reading what designers say about their process and asking them to describe their process is also unsatisfactory for several reasons. The composer Richard Wagner was once asked by a music critic to explain *The Ring* and is said to have replied somewhat testily that 'it is the explanation'. Similarly, most designers are at their best when designing, rather than explaining. Of course, designers must sell their services in the marketplace and so may not always describe their processes honestly! The author's experience of many years of teaching design students also suggests that, when they like a solution, designers are amazingly creative in imagining the 'logical' processes that led to that solution! They are also at times quite capable of denying both to themselves and others the obvious importance of issues which they have chosen either to ignore completely or to relegate to minor consideration.

So what should we do to investigate design? Quite simply, we must do all we can. There is a role for philosophizing about design, we can learn from observation, we might get insight from experiments, and we would be foolish indeed not to try to ask designers how they do it. There are many ways of approaching a study in which designers are asked to describe their process. These would range from questionnaires remotely administered on large samples to in-depth interviews necessarily conducted on rather smaller samples. This book is a contribution to the latter course of action, but with some special qualifications.

It could be argued that it is more useful to know how a few outstanding designers work and think than to conduct experiments on large numbers of less able ones. The designers who appear here are all much admired, and many of them have written theoretical treatises as well as practising. There is certainly no uniform view of architecture presented here, but rather one of high quality. The architects in this book have been chosen to represent a wide variety of backgrounds. They are at different stages in their lives and the development of their careers. They work in different countries and on different sorts of projects. They have expressed varying views about architecture and critics have classified their work in many ways.

Each chapter begins with a very brief biography of the architect or architects concerned and concludes with a very selective bibliography which includes only references the author has found particularly helpful in understanding the way they design. Similarly, the illustrations are selected to help understand the process used rather than to represent the end product, and the architecture shown is not intended to be a comprehensive catalogue of work. It could not be so since each designer could have one or more whole books written about their work, and in some cases this has already happened. These chapters are the result of research into what the architects have written and what others have written about them, but, most importantly, result from discussions between the author and the architects. These chapters then quote what the designers themselves have said during this conversation. Several of our designers do not speak English as their first language, and in any case the discussion was often animated and certainly informal. In spite of this, they have been quoted literally to avoid any danger of the author's interpretation interfering with the meaning of what was being said.

The author has written a more theoretical book *How Designers Think* (Lawson, 1990) to which this can be seen as a companion volume. Many of the key ideas developed in that book were woven into the questions put to the architects reviewed in this book, and so the rest of this intro- duction will be devoted to a brief review of some of those ideas. These can be seen as signposts to some of the questions that might usefully be in the mind of the reader of the main text. Throughout the remaining chapters these issues will be referred to in a column running alongside the main text, and some general conclusions about them are attempted in the final chapter.

We tend to lionize our great designers today and some of their names have become so well known that we can all too easily assume their work to be entirely personal. Of course, this is not so. Not one of the practices taking part in this book is a single-person enterprise, but rather in every case team work is involved. How that team is organized, communicates among its members and with others outside is therefore a legitimate subject for investigation by those who would wish to understand the design process.

By contrast, early writers on the design process tended to see it as a sequence of cognitive operations conducted entirely within one brain. Perhaps due to their own search for order, such writers often favoured models of the process which were based on a series of tasks which, it seems reasonable to suppose, must take place and in a sequence that would appear quite logical. Many models were proposed which relied upon more or less the same central ideas. The design process was generally held to consist of a problem being stated, then analysed, a solution being synthesized and evaluated, followed by a process of communication. This view of design as a sequence of 'assimilation', 'analysis', 'synthesis', 'evaluation' and 'communication' was even reinforced by the Royal Institute of British Architects in its stage model of design practice around which the then standard fee scale was constructed.

Some writers elaborated these models by suggesting the need for 'feedback' loops from one stage to a previous stage if the work had proved unsatisfactory. In particular, of course, it was expected that the 'evaluation' stage may need to be followed by a new 'synthesis'. Others suggested that somehow this whole process was itself iterated at increasing levels of detail as the designer was assumed to move from the general to the particular.

Such models seemed to have an almost unassailable logic and would probably have appeared quite convincing to those not personally involved in the act of designing. However, while the 'methodologists' gathered at conferences to discuss the finer detail of such ideas, designers were quietly ignoring them and getting on with the business of design. While few designers found themselves able to articulate a clear statement about their process, neither did they recognize these oversimplistic models. What cannot be denied is that a designer is unlikely to be successful unless able to generate ideas, that there will be times when analytic thought is appropriate and that a critical and evaluative faculty is essential. What is more questionable is the extent to which these cognitive operations are actually separated into distinct phases, and how the designer controls the necessary shift of mental gears between one and another.

Where, then, do designers begin? What do they do first and why? We might find such a question rather odd if posed to a composer, a painter or a sculptor. It is perhaps our natural wish for tidiness that even suggests to us such an inquiry. The composers of songs, operas and musicals have often been asked a similar type of question. Which comes first, the words or the music? Some have answered, the words, others the music, and some have confessed that it varies. We shall see in this book that the starting point for designers is, if anything, an even more confusing matter.

It is now easy to see why these sequential models of design were doomed to failure. They began from several false premises two of which we need concern ourselves with here. These concern fallacies about both the beginning and the end of design: first, that design problems are, or indeed, can be stated clearly, and second that there are solutions which can be considered in some way optimal. Today we recognize design problems as belonging to a type known as 'wicked'. They are often vague expressions about a change of some kind which is needed or desired rather than a clear statement about a totally defined goal. They should therefore most definitely not be considered to be like crosswords or other popular types of puzzle. These are characterized by a totally defined objective and usually have a single correct solution which can often be recognized as such when it is found. Those who write about the design process as if it were merely problem solving do the field a disservice. A large part of the business of designing involves finding problems, understanding and clarifying objectives and attempting to balance criteria for success. Those who have little knowledge of design often imagine that it starts with a 'brief' presented by a 'client'. This is just one of the ideas that will be tested and found wanting in this book.

Since design problems cannot be comprehensively stated or formulated it follows that they are not susceptible to a method of thorough analysis. The 'analysis, synthesis, evaluation' models of design are again found wanting here. We have now recognized that designers often come to understand their problems through their attempts to solve them. We might call this analysis through synthesis. Laboratory experiments conducted by the author have shown that students of design gradually develop cognitive strategies based upon this procedure, whereas students of natural sciences do not. This was confirmed by interviews conducted with the architects of prize-winning housing schemes (Darke, 1978) from which we developed the notion of the 'primary generator' as a useful way of understanding this process. Here a designer has some basic idea about the form the solution could take and a crude design is predicated on this basis and tested. Sometimes the tests will lead to a refinement of the idea and sometimes to its rejection, but in either case the designer learns more about the problem.

It is clear that designers bring their own concerns into the process. The reader may already know of many of the designers in this book and be able to recognize their particular interests. In some cases these interests and concerns have become clearly articulated outside design work itself, perhaps by the writing of books and articles or through lectures. Indeed, two very important books on the reading lists of today's students of architecture come from designers in this study (Hertzberger, 1991; Venturi, 1977). It is often the case that these ideas form a coherent theory which can be seen to offer what we might call 'guiding principles' which these designers seek to apply when actually designing. In fact, it really turns out to be more of a two-way process and we might more usefully regard design projects as the vehicle for research into these ideas.

It is a reasonable assumption that clients choose architects to some extent because they like earlier designs they have seen. Some clients have a very clear vision of how they want the final design to be, while others may have almost no idea. Some clients are particularly concerned about some features and care little about others. The relationship between client and designer therefore is not like that of an examiner setting students a question but rather more like a someone seeking help in a situation where many courses of action are possible. Inevitably, then, we shall see in this book that the relationship between client and designer can vary greatly but that, at its best, it can be a highly interaction and indeed creative one.

It is quite likely today that those who commission buildings are not actually going to use the buildings themselves. Architects therefore must try to consider the feelings of their 'users' as opposed to their 'clients'. How they do this is now a matter for great debate. Clearly, architects can imagine themselves to be that user, preferring to rely upon their own experience. Others may seek more empirically based evidence and even work with social scientists, or use participatory design methods. Others still seem to have theories of their own invention about what is likely to make the building appeal to people. We shall see a great variety in attitudes towards this issue among the designers in this book.

Design is undoubtedly an artistic business, but it is dangerous to confuse it with art. Most designers see themselves as artistic but not necessarily as artists. Philippe Starck has said that 'I am not an artist, and I don't make art. My aim is to make a better life, a better world, a simple world.' The question of what is or is not art is itself too large to debate here, and perhaps Marshall McLuhan's assertion that 'art is anything you can get away with' will have to do for now! (McLuhan, 1967) However, design usually involves making something that must work in some way as well as expressing some values or ideas. The Modern Movement in architecture was based upon a number of principles, one of the most important of which was 'functionalism'. It was argued that 'form follows function' and that the 'plan is the generator'. This was in some ways a major discontinuity in the historical development of architectural style. It was accompanied by a swing towards the abstract and a concentration on pure form and proportion perhaps exemplified by Mies Van der Rohe's famous aphorism 'less is more'. More recently the pendulum has started to swing back, with more emphasis placed on what architecture signifies and expresses than on its abstract sculptural form. Some theorists have suggested that, in reality, function can sometimes follow form. One of the architects in this book, Herman Hertzberger, has suggested that we should think of form less as a functioning apparatus and more as a (musical) instrument capable of being played upon. Another of the architects in this book, Robert Venturi, has even bowdlerized Mies by suggesting that 'less is a bore' (Venturi, 1977). Although this book is not primarily concerned with such architectural theories they are relevant to our investigation in as much as they influence the design process itself.

Inevitably, the end product of contemporary architectural design often demands that a great deal of technology be employed. The extent to which the problems posed by the technology influence the designer's thoughts is a central issue in understanding the design process. We have passed through a period of the Modern Movement in architecture which itself gave some theoretical basis for an approach to this question. There have been, and still are, those who believe that the technology should be honestly expressed, that buildings should tell us how they stand up and control the environment. However, we shall see that today there is not only a proliferation of architectural theory but also a considerable variation in the way architects regard the role of technology in design.

There are, of course, many other questions about the nature of the design process which we could pose here, and readers will no doubt have their own. However, these few central issues have been raised in order to stimulate the mind into a critical mode before launching into the main body of the book. The rest of the book may be regarded as a mosaic rather than a developing argument. It is a resource for those who wish to study the design process. There is no particular significance to the order of chapters or the sequence of issues raised within each chapter. Readers may wish to read it from cover to cover, follow a particular issue through using the signposts provided by the running-commentary column, or simply delve as the mood takes them. The final chapter tries to bring some of these issues into sharper focus by dealing with them directly and comparing and contrasting the approach of the various designers in the book.

Bibliography

Darke, J. (1978). The primary generator and the design process. In W. E. Rogers and W. H. Ittleson (eds), *New Directions in Environmental Design Research: proceedings of EDRA 9* (pp. 325-337), Washington: EDRA.

Gregory, S. A. (1966). *The Design Method*, London: Butterworths.

Hertzberger, H. (1991). *Lessons for Students in Architecture* (Ina Rike, translator), Rotterdam: Uitgeverij 010.

Lawson, B. R. (1990). *How Designers Think* (second edition), London: Butterworth Architecture.

McLuhan, M. (1967). *The Medium is the Massage*, Harmondsworth: Penguin.

Rittel, H. W. J., and Webber, M. M. (1973). Dilemmas in a general theory of planning. *Policy Sciences*, **4**.

Venturi, R. (1977). *Complexity and Contradiction in Architecture*, New York: The Museum of Modern Art.

Richard Burton

Richard Burton's stepfather was Director General of the Festival of Britain and he thus came into contact with many influential architects at one of the most exciting and intense periods of architectural development seen in the United Kingdom. He met his future partners Peter Ahrends and Paul Koralek at the Architectural Association where they collaborated even as students. Even then they resolved to form a partnership but on leaving the AA in 1956 they split up for several years. After a period in France, Richard Burton spent a year working for the former London County Council before joining Powell and Moya. The partnership eventually got together after Paul Koralek won the competition to design the library for Trinity College in Dublin. Since then the practice has established itself as one of the most consistent producers of high-quality design across a wide range of building types for over 30 years. In more recent years they have acquired another kind of fame following the well-known comments by the Prince of Wales on their competition-winning scheme for the extension to the National Gallery in London, about which they have maintained a dignified silence.

In his early formative years as an architect Richard Burton was heavily influenced by the work of Frank Lloyd Wright and his master, Louis Sullivan. He also developed a keen interest in the sociology of architecture probably dating from his time at the LCC. These ideas came to fruition in his well-published collaboration with the social psychologist, Peter Ellis, in the design of housing at Chalvedon in Essex. He is well known for his highly influential work in raising the issue of energy consciousness on the British architectural agenda with the first serious attempt to develop an energy policy for the profession. These concerns were most convincingly demonstrated in the design of St Mary's Hospital on the Isle of Wight, which was designed to use significantly less energy than a conventional building. He has also worked tirelessly to reintroduce craftsmanship and art into architecture through both his own work and the PerCent for Art scheme. He has recently acted as the chair of a national committee reviewing the future of British architectural education.

Richard Burton has what might be called a pragmatic holistic approach. The span of architectural issues which interest him impressively ranges from the highly technical matters of energy conservation through a deep concern to understand user needs to a burning desire to incorporate more art into architecture. He also talks a great deal about the way the design team works and, in particular, how it relates to the client. This is, however, no abstract intellectual exercise, but rather seems to be the result of a busy and inquiring mind applied over many years to the practical matter of getting things built.[1]

Ahrends Burton and Koralek have their offices around a courtyard in a delightful haven behind an otherwise unprepossessing street in Camden in north London. There is a sense of quiet order about the office that is symptomatic of a practice that knows what it is doing without being complacent. The work of the practice is varied but of high quality. It is difficult to define an ABK style and yet there is a recognizable set of attitudes and values behind all their work.

The original three partners, Peter Ahrends, Richard Burton and Paul Koralek, have worked together for over 25 years, and their relationship seems genuinely to be one in which the whole is greater than the sum of the parts. Every scheme which comes out of the office remains the responsibility of one of these three original and titular partners (there are now three more partners in the firm). The practice has now grown to about 50, a size they have been before and one with which Richard Burton is content. He feels that, at that size, the practice seems 'in balance'.[2] They have no wish to 'expand uncontrollably ... because we like being architects rather than administrators, and we're still drawing which is essential'. In the early years the partners worked together much more closely on the same projects than is the case now. The initial project which launched the practice was the library at Trinity College, Dublin, for which Paul Koralek submitted a competition-winning proposal. From then on the three partners worked on the scheme and collaborated on a number of major projects.

Richard Burton clearly feels that the interaction between members of a design team can be a very important influence on the design process.

The group has a distinct advantage over the individual because ideas can become personal property or one's own intellectual territory. The strength of that territory is considerable, and the difficulty of working alone is often in the breaking of the bonds caused by it. With a group the bonds are broken more easily, because the critical faculty is depersonalised.[3]

In their early years of working the three partners elaborated this idea into a strategy to maintain a freshness of view on each project. They would only allow one to make close contact with the client and one of them would remain substantially 'detached enough to see some twist in the changes of the direction of the inquiry'.

This pattern of working between the partners is less evident in the current larger practice but the emphasis on what Richard Burton calls 'intervention' remains. He lays great stress on using colleagues to give this fresh view on design problems and to intervene in the group to avoid it stagnating:

[1]Guiding principles

It may seem to be a personality trait of the successful designer to be interested in such a wide variety of issues. Certainly it seems important that designers should have open and well-educated minds. Trying to deal with such disparate matters as the physics of energy conservation, the social psychology of group working and the incorporation of art and craftsmanship into architecture may not appeal to those with a rather more convergent personality. There is no question, however, these are all strong guiding principles behind Richard Burton's work and the challenge of resolving them is what drives him on.

[2]Office size and structure

Most of the designers here expressed a view about some notional ideal size of office. This size seems to have something to do with the maximum work load which one of the senior partners can still remain in touch with and perhaps indicates that job satisfaction is more important than purely business-based concerns for such designers.

[3]The design team

Richard Burton has worked with social psychologists to help him to understand the needs of users. It is quite clear, however, that this interest has extended into a study of the workings of the design team as a social organization. Several other designers in this book comment specifically on the value of the team, particularly Richard MacCormac, John Outram and Ken Yeang. Richard Burton has published his own rather more full account of his interesting views on working creatively in groups. (Ahrends, Burton and Koralek, 1971)

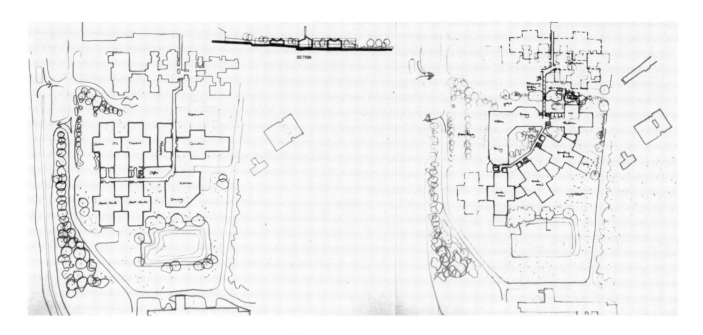

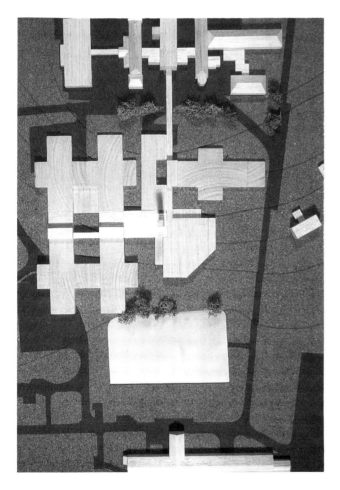
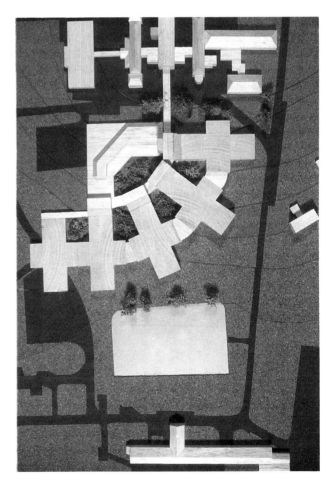

The design team, including not only the architects but also their consultants and representatives of the client, worked for three days on these initial ideas. Three basic planning options were identified on the second day, of which two are shown here. Models were made overnight and on the third day the basic strategy of the design was decided.

To rely continually on common assumptions can be dangerous, not least because it can lead to stagnation, so we welcome intervention, which can be either external or from within the group ... it's essential that the group should not become a small closed community. Indeed we see closed communities as seed-beds of fantasy.[4]

Richard Burton also sees his relationship with the client as critical in the design process. In particular, he stresses the interactive nature of brief making. 'Briefing has become a much more sophisticated thing for us now than it was at one time, and what is interesting is that the clients are beginning to understand that briefing is an absolutely crucial element.' Most of Ahrends Burton and Koralek's buildings are substantial in size and have been designed for large institutional clients such as universities, hospital boards or commercial organizations. This gives rise to a number of issues to which Richard Burton has given considerable attention. First there is the problem of maintaining continuity throughout the necessarily long project. Second, in such cases there is often a remoteness from the actual users of the buildings as opposed to the clients.

Large projects often involve client committees and this leads to problems when the personnel change. 'In government jobs so many people get promoted out of your client body ... and our experience is that at the end of the job we are actually the only people who were there at the beginning.' Richard Burton feels that the higher the level the client contact is in the client organization, the better the process works. He cites the involvement of Terence Conran himself during their work for Habitat. Richard Burton emphasizes the need for clients to understand the complexities of the design process and devote high-level staff continuously to the project. This is understandable given his desire to see the briefing process as 'very much one of to-ing and fro-ing' so that the client can see the drawings and contribute ideas.[5]

Richard Burton works hard to ensure he gets what he calls 'feedback' from the users of his buildings, and, in particular, he has pioneered the use of social psychologists in the design process. Sometimes this 'feedback' is actually after the design is complete 'to improve and inform the quality of further designs', and sometimes it has been in order to 'help formulate the brief'. Burton is somewhat dismissive of the problems of combining the very different processes of empirical social science and of design. Since the exercise is to inform the design process, that consideration clearly dominates in his attitude here, and he talks of 'conditioning' the social psychologists he has worked with. Richard Burton also recognizes that the exercise of consulting users in this way can itself impact on the users, as when designing the Chalvedon housing development with the social psychologist Peter Ellis.[6] 'It was a piece of social psychology, there was a piece of work like that on one hand, but on the other hand it was a piece of social engineering, which wasn't one-way but two-way'.

Richard Burton insists that this kind of work can only be made meaningful as part of a design process if it is interactive. He is rather less enthusiastic about the tendency of some social scientists, such as Newman or Coleman, to conduct user research away from design and then to propose prescriptive formulae for designers to follow. He believes that 'life is a bit more complicated than that ... and working together with people can achieve an enormous amount within this jungle of difficulty'.[7]

[4]Intervention
Richard Burton seems to see the need for an almost institutionalized mechanism for bringing a fresh view into the design process. This is often achieved in schools of design by bringing in visiting critics who have not been involved closely in the student's own design process. It represents the need to break the chain of convergent thought which can lead to a solution forming too quickly. The comments by Richard MacCormac on this subject suggest that he holds very similar views.

[5]The client
Many of the designers in this book emphasize the importance of the client in the design process. Unfortunately, clients are rarely trained for this role. Clearly this is a rather different experience when the client is represented by a large committee as opposed to an individual. Michael Wilford also makes some interesting comments on the client as a committee, while Eva Jiricna represents a designer more used to working closely with individual clients.

[6]The users
A more detailed account of this work was published at the time and it still represents one of the best-documented attempts at involving a social psychologist in the design team (Ellis, 1977). It is worth contrasting this application of formal methods for finding out about the user's views and needs with the more experiential approach favoured by Herman Hertzberger.

[7]Design and science
There is perhaps something of a culture gap here between scientists, particularly of the social variety with their emphasis on correctness of method and the description of phenomena, compared with the rather more prescriptive nature of design, where decisions must be made on a best-guess basis without the luxury of an unlimited period of study. There is also the danger that scientists tend only to look for issues in their own field of study. A good example of this is the building scientist, who can tell you with great apparent precision how much heat is lost through different building materials but is not aware of the amount of heat lost when leaving the back door open to take rubbish out to the bin!

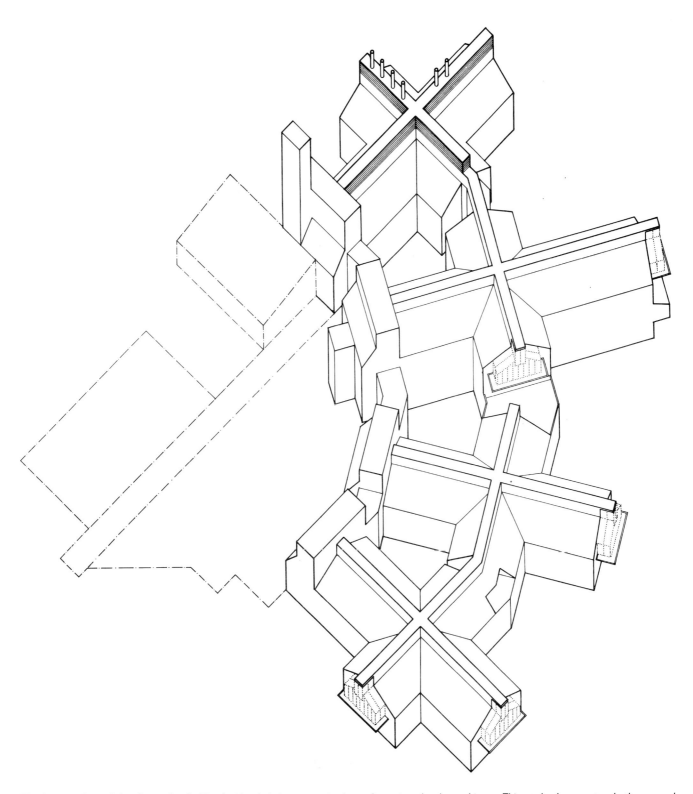

The basic outline of the design for St Mary's Hospital drawn out in three dimensions by the architects. This study shows not only the general arrangement of the wards and circulation but also the section which was adopted.

Richard Burton is an artist as well as an architect, and perhaps therefore it is natural that he should stress the importance of drawing as part of the design process. However, he believes strongly in the role drawing can play in clarifying the thought processes behind design ideas. 'I know now that if I can't visualize a thing clearly in my mind I'm not going to be able to draw it very well, maybe I can draw something, but I can't draw very well.' Being an artist, it clearly offends Richard Burton to draw 'not very well'. In turn he feels this motivates him to visualize better in order to improve the drawing. Thus the urge to produce better drawings drives forward the need to resolve and clarify ideas in his mind.[8]

This close interaction between himself and his drawing leaves Richard Burton personally unenthusiastic about the idea of computer-aided design, of which he makes no use himself. He considers that the directness with which he can alter a drawing is missing when mediated by a computer and thus the feeling is lost. Richard Burton recognizes the advantages of computer-aided drafting which is widely used in ABK, but he remains unconvinced about the computer as a partner in the design process itself.[9]

As well as being an artist Richard Burton is also very much concerned with the technology of architecture. He has campaigned for energy-saving building design and he led the first RIBA energy programme in the late 1970s. Perhaps his most powerful demonstration of these principles is to be seen in the recently completed St Mary's Hospital on the Isle of Wight, which is designed to consume only half the energy normally expected of a building of its kind. Perhaps surprisingly, however, Richard Burton does not see technology as a dominating design generator. Even as early as 1979, when developing the campaign for energy-saving architecture, Richard Burton wrote 'energy in building has had a fanfare lately and maybe it will have to continue for some time, but soon I hope the subject will take its correct place among the 20 other major issues a designer of buildings has to consider'.

Richard Burton thus does not see energy saving or any other technical matter as providing him with a primary generator of design ideas, and he certainly is not interested in technological image making. In St Mary's Hospital the services are all hidden from view in a cleverly conceived section. He argues that in a hospital

you don't want the feeling that you're always in a technological box ... you don't want to be reminded of the entrails. It's like the artery and vein system and the arteries are taking all the services and you don't see them, and the veins and all the workings of the hospital and all the patients and people are in a different system.

Similarly, Richard Burton feels that 'structure's very important, but I think it was overemphasized in our time, when we were being taught ... I think it's only a component, rather like energy'.[10]

In fact Richard Burton sees a major skill for the designer as being the holding in balance of technology and art. He talks of the popular psychological view of the two hemispheres of the cerebral cortex specializing in this way:

There's the poet and the artist on one side and the technician on the other and this is a good metaphor for what we're up to as architects. The danger is when you see only the technical man, or the artist who doesn't have any practical skills. I see the architect is right in the middle trying to hold these two together in a kind of

[8]Drawing
Herman Hertzberger expresses the view that design drawings should not be viewed as art. There is often a confusion about this, since many designers are obviously artistic if not even artists in their own right as is Richard Burton. Clearly, however, Richard Burton here is telling us that the ability to draw as an artist has an effect of forcing him to resolve ideas during his design process. Santiago Calatrava seems to hold similar views about the role and purpose of drawings done during the design process.

[9]Computer-aided design
It is important to distinguish the use of the computer as a drawing tool from its use in the design process. Few of the designers in this book seem very convinced about the latter, with Ian Ritchie and Robert Venturi probably being the most enthusiastic. The comments of Michael Wilford and Santiago Calatrava suggest similar views to those of Richard Burton.

[10]Technology
This is perhaps a surprising view from a designer with such a strong emphasis on technologically correct solutions. Such a position shows great maturity of approach in being able to campaign tirelessly to improve the way architects design building as energy consumers while still appreciating that it must take its place among many other issues. Many other ecological zealots have alienated architects because of their inability to take such a mature view and consequently may even have set back their own cause.

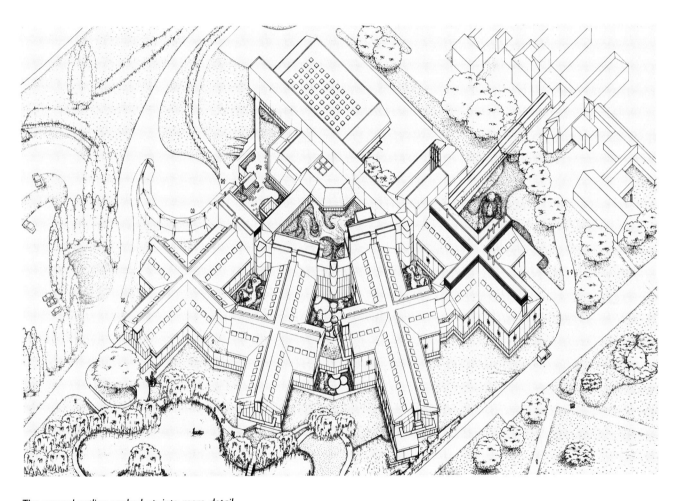

The general outline worked up into more detail.

harmony, and if he gets it right it produces almost another dimension, and if you go into such a building you say 'ah that's it'.[11]

[11]**Art and technology**
See Ian Ritchie's lovely image of the parrots sitting on his shoulders for a similar view.

If any factor can be said to have more of a generative influence on Richard Burton's early design it is probably that of circulation. 'We order our buildings very much by thinking about the way people move. I think if you study our plans we're very involved in the movement patterns in buildings.' But even here Burton warns of the danger of letting this influence dominate in too functional a manner. 'I feel very convinced that although you can have the ordering device of circulation the spaces that you have within the building must have that wonderful repose … you have to get the circulation in proportion.'

Richard Burton does not appear to have much time for architectural symbolism, and certainly this does not feature in his design process. In particular, he feels that architectural jokes and witticisms wear rather thin over the life of a building. His passion for combining art and architecture lead him to an alternative view of the role of symbolic elements in buildings. 'I prefer to have the symbolism not in the architecture but in the more ephemeral things that you can have in a building, like the works of art.' This again reflects Richard's integrated view of both architecture and the design process, with craftsmen and artists being drawn in to interact with the architect as the design proceeds.[12]

[12]**Symbolism**
In this regard Richard Burton seems to agree with Eva Jiricna, who also sees her work as having something of a background quality in front of which appear more temporary but possibly more meaningful images. This can be contrasted in particular with John Outram, who operates a design process guided by considerations of symbolism.

In essence, this could be seen to be very much of a Bauhaus view of design, and indeed Richard Burton still feels the original objectives of the Modern Movement to be valid:

Actually I think Gropius was very outspoken about the very thing I'm talking about. He said 'it's about bringing it all together' and I think the Bauhaus has been misrepresented by many people … seeing the publications and the people who were there, the painters, the sculptors, the furniture designers. It was actually a school about integration, it wasn't a school about separation, so I think it went wrong somewhere else and I suspect it went wrong in England after the Second World War when we were taken over by people who were trying to scrimp and save.

Along with this strong sense of integration Richard Burton also feels the design process must work quickly. This follows from his insistence that no one aspect of the problem should dominate. From his teaching and examining experience he identifies a failure to work quickly enough as one of the problems facing students trying to develop their own design process.[13] Certainly Richard Burton's own design process appears to be an extremely challenging intellectual exercise. It is essentially a team exercise involving interaction between designers, clients and consultants. Richard Burton brings a very wide agenda of deeply felt personal concerns to the process, ranging from the highly technical to the explicitly artistic, and yet perhaps the most passionate concern is not to allow any one issue to dominate. He likes to shift very quickly between all the relevant constraints, and this involves very careful preparation in terms of assembling the necessary information and expertise.

[13]**Speed of working**
Richard Burton lays great emphasis on this need for speed in order to cycle round all the issues which he feels an architect must maintain in balance. The images of the designer as a juggler used by Richard MacCormac and Michael Wilford seem to advance similar arguments.

A good example of this process can be seen in the way ABK tackled the design of the St Mary's Hospital. Richard Burton assembled a substantial team of people in the ABK office for three days to work on the early design stage. There were representatives of the three client bodies, the national, regional and district health authorities, members of the ABK design team and their consultants. A great deal of groundwork had been

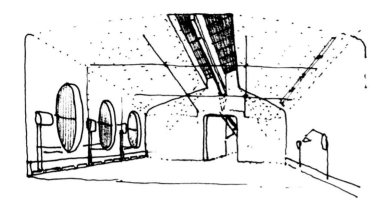

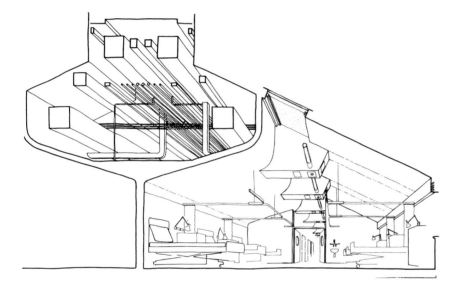

The concept for the section used in the ward blocks is shown here developing from an early sketch, through a more detailed section, to a photograph of the finished building.

done before the meeting. The site had been extensively analysed and a decision had already been taken to use the 'nucleus templates' for a number of the departments.

On the first day they generally agreed the main headings of the brief, and by the end of the second day they had already identified three basic planning options, including the curved form finally adopted. Models were made that night and the next day the architects and clients worked together on choosing the final option which was already roughly costed. Although clearly many planning changes were to follow, the basic scheme appears not to have altered substantially.[14] Richard Burton believes that this sort of process only works given several important attitudes. 'I believe in moving quite fast ... accepting that you go for a series of options ... being willing to accept the whole, but being willing to say after a bit of time, "no we've made a mistake".'

So far, the St Mary's Hospital appears to be pleasing the client, has had extremely favourable feedback from the residents of the island, is receiving widespread favourable architectural criticism, and looks like meeting its energy-saving targets. The design process used clearly demands a team of highly educated and experienced designers, and it is worth noting that Richard Burton has recently turned his attention to the future pattern of architectural education in the United Kingdom.

[14]**Alternatives**

Again there are similarities here with both Eva Jiricna and Michael Wilford, both of whom describe their process as being the generation of a range of alternatives from which a selection is made. All three are involved in teaching and identify this skill as one of the most difficult for the student to acquire. However, this is not a uniformly held view, and Richard MacCormac, Santiago Calatrava and Ken Yeang are at the other end of the spectrum of opinion in this book.

Some of Richard Burton's sketches for a housing scheme.

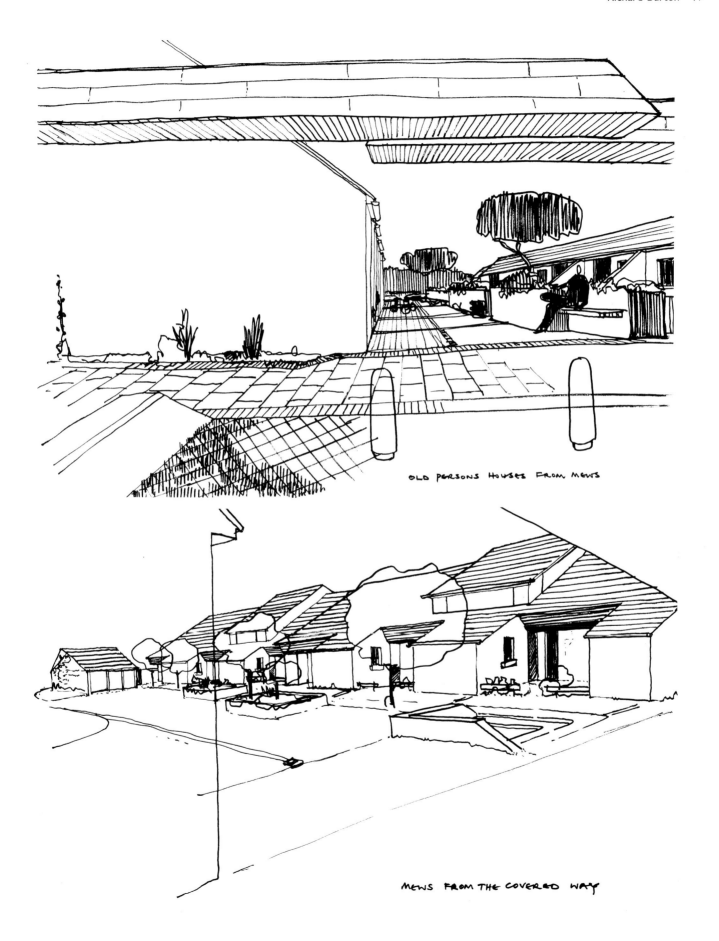

OLD PERSONS HOUSES FROM MEWS

MEWS FROM THE COVERED WAY

Richard Burton

Bibliography

Ahrends, P., Burton, R., and Koralek, P. (1991). *Ahrends, Burton and Koralek.*, London: Academy Editions.

Baker, N. (1990). A machine for healing: ABK's St Mary's Hospital. *Architecture Today*, **9**, 35–52.

Broadbent, G. (1977). Chalvedon: Sociology's contribution minimal? *Architects' Journal*, **166**(37), 785.

Burton, R., Ahrends, P., and Koralek, P. (1971). Small group design and the idea of quality. *RIBA Journal*, **78**(6), 232–239.

Burton, R., & O'Sullivan, P. (1977). Energy and the profession. *RIBA Journal*, **84**(10), 430–432.

Burton, R. (1979). Energy in buildings. *Architects' Journal*, **170**(44), 922.

Davey, P. (1991). St. Mary's. *Architectural Review*, **189**(1128), 24–33.

Davies, C. (1991). Hospitality. *Architects' Journal*, **194**(1), 24–31.

Dormer, P. (1990). Out of the woods. *World Architecture*, **2**(4), 64–67.

Ellis, P. (1977). Chalvedon housing area, Basildon: a social psychological evaluation. *Architects' Journal*, **166**(37), 488–494.

Ellis, P. (1978). Social Sciences, user research and the design process. *Architects' Journal*, **167**(6), 248.

Wright, L. (1967). Library at Trinity College Dublin. *Architects' Journal*, **146**(15), 903–922.

Wright, L. (1974). Extrovert library: Maidenhead library, Berkshire. *Architectural Review*, **155**(927), 256–267.

Santiago Calatrava

Santiago Calatrava is one of an extremely rare breed of architect–
engineers, being qualified in both professions and practising at the
junction between them. He was born in 1951 in the town of Benimamet
in the Spanish region of Valencia. He grew up there, going to evening
classes in Arts and Crafts as early as the age of eight. After leaving school
he attended the local art college, and then studied architecture at the
Escuela Tecnica Superior de Arquitectura de Valencia. His studies briefly
moved up to the urban scale and with an apparently unquenchable thirst
for knowledge he moved to Switzerland to study civil engineering in
Zurich. He continued to pursue an academic career with research into
foldable frameworks, for which he was awarded his doctorate in 1981.
Eventually he set up his own office to practise both architecture and civil
engineering in Zurich, where he is still based, although he now also has
an office in Paris.

Santiago Calatrava seems as much at ease working at the scale of
jewellery or sculpture as he does when designing large bridges or railway stations. In fact his work includes buildings, street furniture, civil
engineering and intermediate structures such as canopies. His approach
defies categorization in that his engineering is highly sculptural and his
architecture exploits the power of innovative but logical structural form.
Underlying all his work at whatever scale is a consistent attempt to make
structural form expressive and appropriate. The influence of his early life
in Valencia and more recent years in Switzerland can perhaps be seen in a
totally new approach to form, which appears to combine and develop the
traditions of Gaudi and Maillart.

However, in reality, the first decade of Santiago Calatrava's work must
now be considered in its own right. He has already won many prizes in
design competitions and has built a considerable number of projects. His
work has begun to be widely published and he has recently mounted a
major retrospective exhibition at the Royal Institute of British Architects in
London and has been awarded the Gold Medal by the Institute of Civil
and Structural Engineers.

The architectural and engineering practice of Santiago Calatrava employs about 40 staff at offices in Zurich and Paris.[1] Although Dr Calatrava lives in Paris, which has the larger of the two offices, it is perhaps the smaller office in the old part of Zurich which represents the heart of the operation. It was here that Santiago Calatrava first began to practise after completing his studies at the university. He had visited Switzerland frequently in his childhood and clearly feels a considerable affinity not only with the country but with Zurich itself. It is perhaps partly the quietness of what is nevertheless a cosmopolitan European city which appeals to Calatrava. He remains an essentially rather private man who devotes his life largely to his family and his work. Indeed his wife and brother-in-law, although neither architects nor engineers, are closely involved in the organization of his working life and of the practice, leaving Calatrava himself free to concentrate on design. He speaks of dedicating his work to members of this close family, which perhaps gives him the stability and continuity that allows him to be so revolutionary and experimental in his work.

The practice in Zurich also represents a fascinating symbiosis of European cultures which appears to be extremely important in the way Calatrava designs. His own background, growing up in Valencia, opened him up to the visually iconoclastic work of the Surrealists and of that most sculptural of architects, Antonio Gaudi. However, counterbalancing this experimental influence he also seems to feed off the precision and attention to detail for which the Swiss are so renowned. In particular, Calatrava's relationship with his model maker is absolutely critical and central to his design process.

Calatrava's work has already attracted enough attention to have been subjected to extensive critical analysis. It is tempting to follow the obvious conclusions about the influences on him through Gaudi and Candela. While Calatrava clearly admires Gaudi he feels this is rather more a background influence than the critics suggest. 'Between Gaudi and our time a lot of important things have happened in terms of technical developments and our understanding of form ... I cannot really explain the influence of Gaudi on my work, but I feel it is because sometimes we went to common sources.' In fact Santiago Calatrava has also absorbed and draws upon rather less well-known Swiss engineering traditions. For example, the raking supports for his Stadelhofen Station in Zurich can be seen as a reference to Gaudi, whereas in fact Calatrava was merely adapting the highly rational Swiss way of using slanting pillars as a road or track enters a tunnel cut into a rockface.

In fact in conversation Calatrava reveals a dazzling array of influences and interests, talking about many architects, engineers, sculptors, painters and even film directors. Paradoxically, he makes many references to the work of Louis Kahn, with whom he is not normally associated by the critics. It is probably an interest in light and his concern with the nature and inherent characteristics of building materials which he shares with Kahn rather than his use of form. 'Concrete is concrete and steel is steel even if it is painted.' This leads Calatrava to explore the nature of materials by contrasting them within a project perhaps unusual today at the scale of large engineering structures, but he freely acknowledges the historical influence of Viollet-le-Duc. He has explored this theme through a series of sculptures in stone and steel, which can be seen to have generated ideas for his bridges:

[1] **Office size and structure**
Compared with the other practices in this book this seems rather large. However, it must be remembered that there are not only two offices in different countries but also that they are responsible for both architectural and engineering work.

A model of the proposed completion of the Cathedral of St John the Divine in New York, which was presented for an invited competition. The programme included a new element in the form of a bioshelter which was placed immediately below the glazed steel roof.

The subsequent illustrations show a series of pages from Santiago Calatrava's sketchbooks. The sketches are all in sequence but with many gaps. Several sketchbooks are worked on in parallel and selections from two of them are shown here.

As well as showing the emergence of the main ideas of the scheme, these sequences also demonstrate several characteristics of Calatrava's process. These include the use of parallel small sketchbooks, the central role of the section, and the use of model making. The guiding principles of 'dynamic equilibrium' and contextual response are also readily apparent.

Early pages from the first sketchbook.

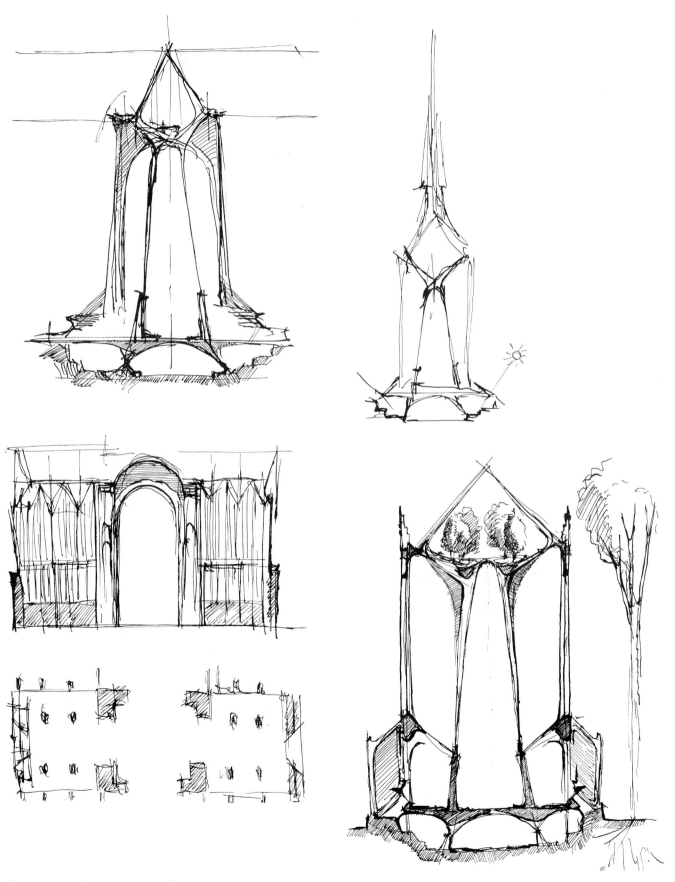

Further sketches from the first sketchbook.

For me the antagonism between materials, especially materials like steel and a material like concrete or stone creates a simple dualism which you can see sometimes in the sculptures. I have done this with two or three materials hitting each other ... but this is a very old thing.[2]

Another popular view of Calatrava is that he draws heavily on organic form. It is true that he makes many sketches not only of the human frame but also of other animals. However, Calatrava denies that he is an organisist as such but rather uses organic form primarily to learn about structural issues. It is clear from Calatrava's early academic work and from his sculptures as well as his engineering structures that he is fascinated by the problem of equilibrium. His doctorate on moving and folding structures also raised issues which still fascinate him. It is the capacity of the skeleton, not only to support the body but also to flex and take on changing distributions of loading that most interests Calatrava. Thus it is not an attempt to imitate natural form for the sake of form which drives Calatrava but rather what he can learn about dynamic balancing structures.[3]

Calatrava is an accomplished artist with a fine sense of line and texture. He is a prolific drawer, but one senses that his graphical output is never the result of a wish to produce a drawing but rather to understand a problem. He seldom works at a drawing table but usually on rather small pads of paper perhaps at about A3 size. 'I could take a big piece of paper and draw the whole thing, but I prefer to concentrate.'[4] His design process depends heavily on a stream of graphical output, sometimes pencil sketches, often water colours, which he uses to communicate his ideas to his staff. He sees this very much as journey of exploration with each sketch following on from its predecessors as the ideas develop. 'You are discovering the layers of your project ... I mean to start with you see the thing in your mind and it doesn't exist on paper and then you start making simple sketches and organizing things and then you start doing layer after layer ... it is very much a dialogue.' He likes to have pads or books of paper in front of him so he can see how far he has got down this journey. In general, he progresses from very early evocative sketches down to the later highly detailed work which is one of the hallmarks of so many of his projects. 'The first sketches are looking at whether you want something high or low ... the last ones are maybe of bolts or pipes and the connections between things.'

Perhaps one of the most surprising lessons to be learned from a study of Calatrava's sketches is how two-dimensional they are. One might expect that an architect who so consistently rejects the orthogonal in favour of what he likes to refer to as 'plastic' form as Calatrava would draw many perspectives, but this is not so. 'When I started as a student I used to exercise in perspective, and I like to draw them in my own time, but I have discovered that to draw perspectives is to be untrue, because the reality is always much better than any perspective!' In fact Calatrava seems to favour the section more than any other view. He works freehand but roughly to scale and often in water colour. The use of colour, however, is rarely figurative. 'The difference in colour is to indicate a difference in material, it can be blues and violets and so on, and then shades to show the light.' These sections consequently have a remarkably three-dimensional feel to them and simultaneously communicate both construction and space. Calatrava feels that perspectives are 'to let someone else see and not for yourself'.[5]

[2] **Materials**
This view about the natural grammar which building materials generate seems similar to that held by Eva Jiricna. However, as we shall see later in this chapter, Calatrava does not use materials as a way of generating alternative designs in the way Eva Jiricna does. The idea of materials having their own characteristics and deliberately contrasting these and highlighting this through the detailing of junctions is definitely a common theme. It is possible that the engineering education received by both Jiricna and Calatrava may have something to do with this elevation of the detail junction to such an important role in the design process.

[3] **Guiding principles**
It is hardly surprising that Calatrava's process depends so heavily on the development of structural forms. Not only is he a fully qualified engineer but most of his work has been at the scale of large structures such as bridges and railway stations. However, this is not always so, and he shows a similar approach when designing small canopies or even furniture and light fittings. What in fact we see here is a major continuing agenda of discovery about a phenomenon, which we might call dynamic equilibrium, explored through work designed at a whole variety of scales and for many purposes.

[4] **Drawing**
These comments show a quite remarkable similarity to those of Herman Hertzberger and Michael Wilford. The size of paper used coincides exactly as does the attitude towards the drawing as a tool rather than an end product. Denise Scott Brown's description of Robert Venturi's drawings as 'never done as works of art but as communication with self' seems to reflect the same view.

[5] **Perspectives**
It is interesting that someone so clearly capable of producing beautiful drawings should also be so cautious about the perspective drawing. Again there is a similarity with Hertzberger's views. It is almost as if the designer is saying, 'Look I can produce seductive views but these can be dangerous while the design is developing'. The extensive use of the section is something that Calatrava shares to some extent with Eva Jiricna. Both seem more interested in and concerned with the vertical dimension rather than the plan.

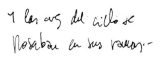

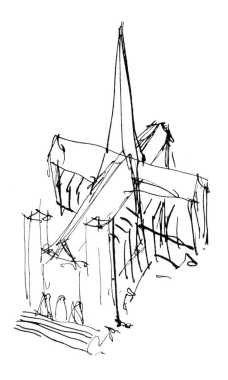

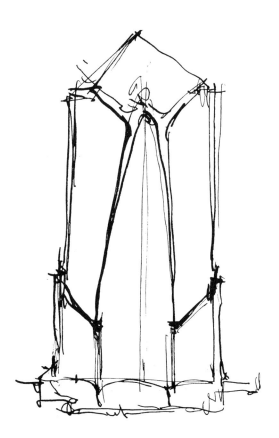

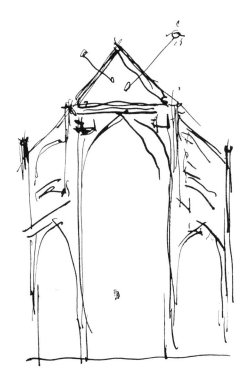

Early pages from the second (smaller) sketchbook.

If Calatrava makes little use of perspectives then this is perhaps also partly because he relies so extensively on the physical model. Calatrava's models come in two kinds: the magnificent and impressive presentation models which made such an impression in his recent retrospective exhibition at the RIBA, and the working models made for exploratory purposes during the design process. All these models are made in a model maker's workshop just a few narrow streets away from the Calatrava office in Zurich. Very rarely does Calatrava use simple linear form and modelling his complex and subtle curves would defeat all but the most skilled craftsman. In this case there is also clearly a deep mutual respect and understanding that allows Calatrava the luxury of having models made even before accurate scale drawings are available:

Sometimes you know it is very difficult to explain through the drawing board or by a sketch that maybe something has to turn around perhaps with a double curve on top ... I would say that the language I have developed with the model maker is very much related to these things and to models, and I can only do this because he is not a simple man, he is someone who is very gifted and enthusiastic.[6]

This attitude towards and respect for craftsmen reveals several other aspects of Calatrava's working methods. He thinks it necessary to 'feel' his way forward in a manner which requires him to draw by hand. The practice does, of course, have computers which are essential for the engineering calculations made necessary by Calatrava's adventurous shapes. He also respects the precision in computer drafting, which in turn he finds useful in the design process, but he seldom uses the computer as a visualization tool:

I very much like the unbelievable precision ... maybe sometimes you want an arc between two points which you want to see immediately and you could not do this by hand ... but for relating reality I don't use the computer much ... I don't like hyper-realistic models I prefer the abstraction of black and white models.[7]

Calatrava is fascinated by the creative possibilities of playing with the effects of scale when using models and sculptures in the design process. 'The change of scale can be a beautiful pattern of creativity.'[8] He is very much aware that a model can communicate geometry, proportion and organization but is often inadequate as a medium for revealing the impact of the full-size object. 'Exploring the first idea of the design in a model is, in my opinion, very important because it gives you the first contact with that future reality.' Calatrava is conscious of the dangers of designing the model rather than the real full-size object, a danger all too real in his case thanks to the amazingly beautiful and precise craftsmanship of his model maker:

I have learnt to appreciate the models as autonomous things, a model is beautiful because a model can be beautiful. It is a certain guarantee that the building will be also, but only a small guarantee ... The model is important therefore in a certain period of the design process but after that we don't look very much at the model, sometimes we come back to remember what we wanted ... I mean it is the end of the first phase of the design process.

For Calatrava, design is largely a linear process. He does not normally believe in exploring alternatives and seems to arrive at the basic idea of a scheme fairly early on. For him this starting point can be remarkably

[6]Models
Santiago Calatrava has collaborated for many years with Domeng Raffeiner, who runs the Zabarowski firm of model makers in Zurich. A visit to the workshop shows just how close and vital the relationship is. Prototypical models at varying scales with successive refinements offer clear evidence of an investigation of the design which is a central feature of Calatrava's process. The superb exhibition models which go on public display are, like presentation drawings, the conclusion of this process. The enthusiasm for the design is shared by those who work on the models to such an extent that one can only conclude that they see themselves as contributing to the design process. I am particularly grateful to Domeng Raffeiner for allowing me to visit his workshop, without which, I believe, no understanding of Santiago Calatrava's work would be complete.

[7]Computer-aided Design
This is an interesting view about computer-aided design since it comes from one who is clearly extremely numerate and capable of using computers. It is sometimes argued that the real problems in CAD are about making the interface more suitable for use by those less naturally inclined to computers. Calatrava appears quite happy to use computers where he finds them useful, for structural calculations and precise drafting. He simply does not find them capable of sustaining the conversation he wishes to have with his drawing, to use Donald Schon's phrase. This view is similar to that expressed strongly by Michael Wilford and, to some extent, by Richard Burton and Richard MacCormac, but contrasts with the views of Ian Ritchie, John Outram and Robert Venturi.

[8]Scale
I am particularly grateful to Anthony Tischauser for pointing out just how much Calatrava uses a change of scale in his design process. An examination of his work reveals similar forms used at the scale of a lamp, a canopy or even a bridge. What Calatrava seems to be telling us here is that by changing scale one can 'see' a form differently and understand it in a new way.

Later pages from the first sketchbook.

fundamental. 'Sometimes it is just a gesture or an idea perhaps about equilibrium, for example.' He feels that to explore too many alternatives is a sign of doubt and that since, sooner or later, the designer must fight for his idea he must believe in it to the exclusion of all else. 'You have to let an idea run and proceed with it to be convinced ... of course you criticise it and you may leave it and start again with something new, but it is not a question of options, it is always a linear process.'[9]

Santiago Calatrava likes to work rapidly and intensively at certain stages of the design process. His staff have learned to recognize the moment when he feels it necessary to devote concentrated effort to a particular project. He believes that design should have a 'freshness and spontaneity' which only come from this intensive method of working, another reason for his lack of enthusiasm for CAD:

I like to sketch quickly by hand, sometimes even on the site, but not using an orthodox drawing table ... the first rough sketch is extremely important ... there are phases sometimes in a project that are extremely intensive, but then to allow the project to mature you must give it time and perhaps change it many times.

Calatrava talks a great deal about the tensions between the intense and relaxed periods of design[10] and between the need to fight for the idea and yet to allow criticism of it. 'On the one hand it needs a lot of spontaneity and on the other it needs perseverance.' Clearly this is an extremely personal matter for him and the process in his office is centred around his personal control of these forces. 'I am the author of the great idea and I am the only one who supports the great idea right through until the end, and in my opinion it is necessary to be very strong, and then sometimes you have to let things float a little bit.'[11]

Although Calatrava is without doubt a great artist and his work is highly personal he is not frustrated, as might be expected by a process which necessarily involves so many other people. In fact it seems it is precisely because his design process involves so much cooperation and communication that makes it so rewarding to him.[12] He explains this through a joke that if the painter Raphael had lost both his arms he could still have been a very good architect. 'The working instrument of the architect is not the hand, but the order, or transmitting a vision of something.' Calatrava sees his design sketches not as works of art, which many of them undoubtedly are, but rather as ways of 'communicating to others so that they may work faster to realize the idea'.[13]

The 'central idea' is critically important to Calatrava, and the understanding of it and its exploration are perhaps for him the whole purpose of the design process. He speaks of the idea being not inside but outside him as some sort of distant light which offers a target or focus for the process. These ideas are often explored through abstract sculptures:

It is very good to do a sculpture because you can have it at home and look at it every night, you can meditate on it and turn it. This is the only quiet moment in the whole process to bring a project to realization ... this focus is very important because it gives you a certain authority ... you can also show it to people and they understand.

Yet Calatrava is essentially a designer rather than a sculptor. He points out that technical advances usually come when we try to solve specific problems rather than from generalized or abstract thought. 'It is the

[9]Alternatives
This rather linear and developmental approach seems nearest to Richard Mac-Cormac, and in considerable contrast to Richard Burton, Eva Jiricna and Michael Wilford, who believe strongly in developing alternative ideas. Denise Scott Brown offers an interesting explanation of this variation.

[10]Speed of working
A number of our designers here raised this idea of the need to change pace in the design process. This corresponds with findings in the literature on creativity. Richard MacCormac also made specific reference to the need to alternate between periods of intense activity and quiet reflection. One of the key problems facing design practice principals is just how to manage their time so that these kinds of periods can be found in what is an otherwise busy schedule. See also Ian Ritchie's and Herman Hertzberger's comments on working quietly at home at night as one way of managing this.

[11]The central idea
This is a fascinating problem at the heart of design management. On the one hand, there is this well-recognized need to defend the 'big idea' against all the forces of compromise which tend to weaken design ideas. On the other, is the need to allow criticism and draw in the contributions of others, who may just have a different perspective and thus generate an even better idea. The early practice of Ahrends, Burton and Koralek provided an interesting way of managing social interaction within the design team specifically to address this problem.

[12]The design team
Calatrava seemed to be talking about the thrill one gets from a group activity which cannot be replicated through individual effort. This peculiar frisson is known, for example, to those who play music in groups or are part of a sports team, and seems to come from the very fact that the group is able to perform together as a result of some understanding which they share but which may not necessarily be made explicit to others outside the group.

[13]Drawing
Again Calatrava is rather humble and dismissive about his drawings. Again we see this concern not to allow design drawings to take over. See the earlier note on this.

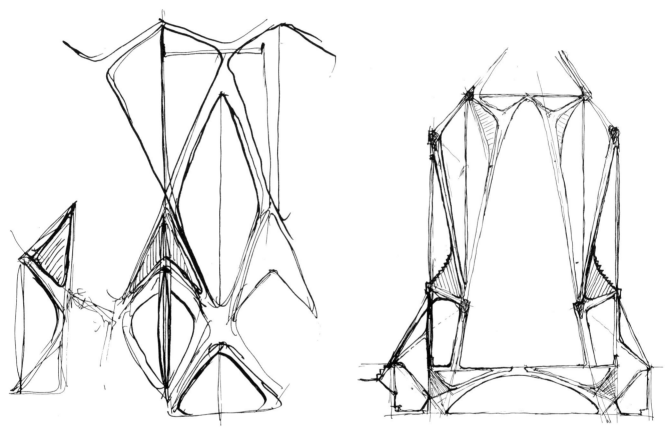

Later pages from the first sketchbook.

answer to a particular problem that makes the work of the engineer ... I can no longer design just a pillar or an arch, you need a very precise problem, you need a place.'[14] He describes how his proposed bridge for the East London crossing grew out of a response to the landscape combined with a study of the technical needs for a wide navigation channel and a height restriction imposed by the approach path to the London City Airport. 'You can justify the solution by itself but also it speaks with the landscape.' Calatrava talks also of how he tries to express ideas and values which he feels appropriate to the context of his work. He feels that his personal joy at the democratization of Spain was something he could celebrate through his bridges there, but that the language of his work in Zurich, and more recently at Lyon, must inevitably be different.[15]

Santiago Calatrava then represents a fusion of the worlds of the civil engineer, the architect and the sculptor. He claims that his imaginative structures do not necessarily cost more to build, but admits they may take longer to design. He feels that to design too quickly and only to look for the cheapest solution is both short-sighted in that this can destroy important landscapes, and often not even an economical policy in terms of lifecycle costs. Most of his work has been commissioned by public authorities who have been convinced by these arguments. Calatrava is trying to make public places which enhance peoples lives. 'Art can also be in public places, it can be on the streets ... and it can bring optimism to people, this aspect should always be considered.'

[14]**Reality and innovation**

This is a most interesting view on innovation which seems to connect with the writings of many other inventors. This is the sort of argument which can be used to defend extra-ordinarily extravagant engineering exercises such as space travel and Formula One motor racing. Many quite fundamental breakthroughs seem to occur through solving quite specific real-world practical problems. New materials and engineering techniques are thus often not the result of pure research but of very applied design. This, in turn, leads to the argument that design is in itself a research-based activity and that all designs are, in that sense, a contribution to knowledge. This view is only just beginning to be sympathetically received in universities, who tend to hold a rather conventional view of research and knowledge. Robert Venturi also expresses similar views about these matters.

[15]**Formal and symbolic**

Calatrava is particularly concerned here to explain the need to balance these two important forces in design. It seems that he has found his own personal way of achieving this by having a continuing programme of the exploration of the formal properties of materials and geometrical systems, but beginning each project by thinking in almost gestural terms about its context. The acclaim with which his work is greeted seems to indicate that he has this balance about right in order to appeal to our senses.

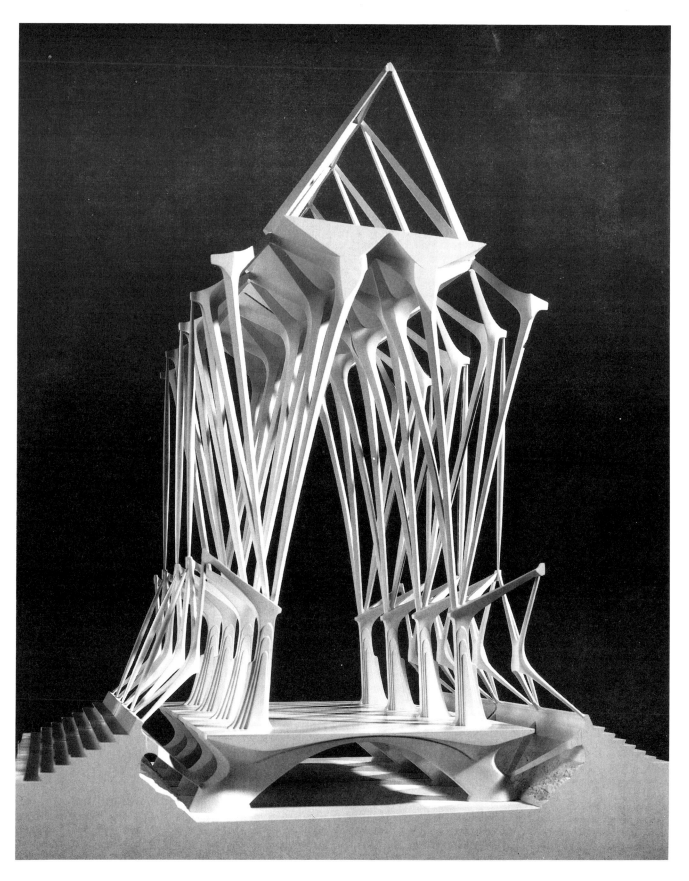

A model of the main structure in an early stage.

Santiago Calatrava

Bibliography

Buchanan, P. (1987). Expressive engineering: Calatrava. *Architectural Review*, **182**(1087), 50–61.

Candela, F. (1992). Calatrava's graceful shapes. *World Architecture*, (13), 46–57.

Harbison, R. (1992). *Creatures from the Mind of the Engineer: the architecture of Santiago Calatrava*, Zurich: Artemis.

Ortelli, L. (1985). The art of science: notes on the work of Santiago Calatrava. Lotus International, **45**, 28–39.

Peters, T. F. (1989). Santiago Calatrava profile. *Progressive Architecture*, **70**(4), 98–103.

Rastorfer, D. (1986). The structural art of Santiago Calatrava. *Architectural Record*, **174**(9/8), 130–139.

Sharp, D. (ed.). (1992). *Santiago Calatrava*, London: Book Art.

Stroud, A. (1991). Conversation with Calatrava. *Concrete Quarterly*, Spring, 22–25.

Herman Hertzberger

Herman Hertzberger was born in Amsterdam in 1932. He was educated at the Technical University of Delft, where he graduated in 1958, immediately starting his own private practice. Herman Hertzberger's practice has designed seminal buildings incorporating his ideas, including a number of schools, old people's housing, the celebrated Centraal Beheer office building in Appledorn and the Vredenburg Music Centre in Utrecht. Perhaps his most famous work, the building for Central Beheer completed in 1972, most succinctly expresses his views about architecture. He has continued to show concern for those who inhabit his buildings in a manner which reveals a deep understanding of the fundamentally important contribution the built environment makes to the lives of ordinary people. Hertzberger's buildings have received many prizes and have been widely published, including exhibitions at both the Paris and Venice Biennales.

Herman Hertzberger has always been a thinker and writer as well as a practising architect, and in 1959 he began the highly influential Dutch architectural magazine *Forum*, which he edited with several others, including Jaap Bakema and Aldo van Eyck. Through *Forum* Herman Hertzberger was able to develop and publish his ideas on 'structuralism' in architecture. He has argued that function should be seen as much a response to form as opposed to the other way round. He developed the idea that architectural form should be thought of as an instrument capable of allowing for individual interpretation by its users rather than as an apparatus capable of single limited use. Most recently he has published his widely acclaimed *Lessons for Students in Architecture*, which is already influencing the next generation of architects. In fact so much has been written by and about Herman Hertzberger that he has already become a major figure playing on the stage which is the history of architecture.

He has taught at the Universities of Amsterdam, Delft and Cambridge, as well as at many in the United States, including the MIT. He is now also Dean at the Berlage Institute, which he has set up in a section of Aldo van Eyck's famous orphanage in Amsterdam.

Herman Hertzberger has an office in central Amsterdam, which, consistent with his structuralist philosophy, is converted from an old house. Amsterdam, with its combination of neatly organized transportation infrastructure in the form of canals, roads and trams, together with its relaxed attitude towards behaviour, is perhaps a nice metaphor for Herman Hertzberger's own work.

This is not the place to rehearse Hertzberger's philosophy of architecture in full since here we concentrate on his process rather than his actual architecture. However, any discussion of Herman Hertzberger's work which is not informed by some understanding of the impact of his architectural interpretation of structuralism is likely to be less than complete. Structuralism to Herman Hertzberger implies that a building should be seen as an instrument to be used by people in a way that allows for their own expression:

There is this idea about language, the fact that you have a structure which is valuable for everybody but is used in different ways. This is illustrated by the warehouses in this town, which were perfectly appropriate for their function when they were built and turned out to be able to become exquisite houses.[1]

Similarly, Herman Hertzberger sees his conversion of part of Aldo Van Eyck's famous orphanage into the Berlage Institute School of Architecture as a compliment to Van Eyck's work:

I cannot believe that the orphanage ever worked better as a home for children than it does now as a school of architecture. In that sense the orphanage is a very structuralist building, perhaps one of the very first.

Herman Hertzberger has a small office which grows and shrinks 'like a stomach' up to 20 in total but has only five or six architects. He also uses 'satellite working' by having links with other practices, and by making extensive use of specialists. Herman Hertzberger himself originates the design.[2] 'I start, I am the only one who starts to formulate the idea.'[3] He always uses A3 size drawing pads:

It's a sort of imperative for me, you know. I insist upon having my concentration on quite a small area, like a chess player. I could not imagine playing chess in an open place with big chequers.[4]

The office is full of these A3 sheets which clearly show his method of working and through which he communicates with his staff. He usually appoints one of his staff as a design assistant for each job early on, and the design team grows as the job progresses. The team also produce A3 drawings which Herman Hertzberger himself takes home and traces over to refine the ideas, returning the sheets the next day. 'For some time we communicate like this handing in and out these A3 sheets. Well, of course, we have a discussion but not very long, maybe a quarter of an hour.'

Herman Hertzberger tries to keep his staff for as long as possible and clearly establishes a small core of dedicated followers who obviously develop a sympathetic understanding of his way of working. He stresses the importance of reducing things down to manageable problems.[5] The A3 pad is a good example of this, but the principle runs through much of his description of his process. He likes to begin with a simple brief, if possible described on one of his sheets. 'You have people in the office

[1] Guiding principles
Herman Hertzberger's structuralist principles have guided his work throughout a distinguished career. Indeed, some of his buildings stand as symbols for that set of principles, perhaps most notably the Centraal Beheer office building in Appledorn which Hertzberger himself described as an 'hypothesis'. This nicely illustrates the two-way interaction between 'guiding principles' and designs with each informing the other, and suggests that we should see the design process as a form of research, and its end products as contributions to knowledge. See also, particularly, the comments by Robert Venturi and Denise Scott Brown and by Ken Yeang on this topic.

[2] Office size and structure
This perhaps seems rather small compared with other practices in this book. It is clear, however, that this practice is a highly personal one and that Herman Hertzberger himself is also involved in teaching. The use of a relatively small core of long-term staff, allowing the office to grow and shrink and cooperating with other practices, all enable Herman Hertzberger to find his own way of keeping close to his work.

[3] The design team
This is a further indication of the extent to which Herman Hertzberger's practice is very personal to him. This is hardly surprising, since the design practice clearly represents an important outlet through which Hertzberger can develop his ideas along with writing and teaching. A similar relationship between the principal and the design team can be found in the chapter on Santiago Calatrava. It is worth comparing Hertzberger's approach in which he clearly gives a design lead with that of Michael Wilford, who sees himself as an 'editor'.

[4] Drawing
This preference for small design drawings is shared with Santiago Calatrava and Michael Wilford.

[5] The brief
Like Michael Wilford and Ken Yeang, Herman Hertzberger likes to start by reducing the brief to the bare minimum.

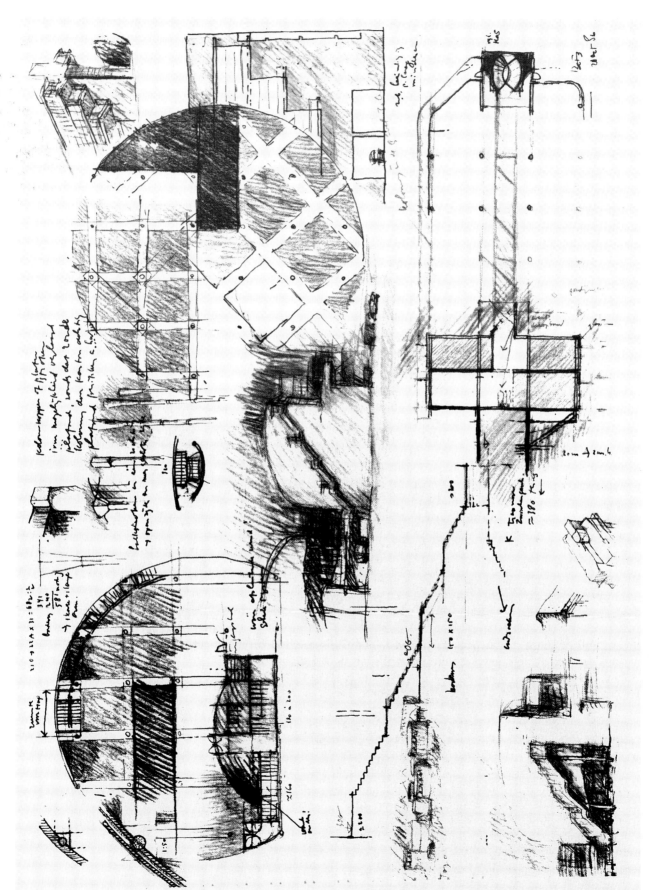

A page from Herman Hertzberger's A3 sketchbook, showing his design for a Film Institute in Berlin. His guiding principles of 'structuralism' are apparent in the organization of grids combined with a study of detailed junctions.

who make things more complicated than they are and others that make it simpler than it is, and I prefer the last one.'

Herman Hertzberger begins to think three-dimensionally from the very beginning but about what he calls 'proto-form' which is 'not the form it will take in the end'. He agrees that architects always think in terms of form, 'but most of the time too soon [in the process]'. For Herman Hertzberger even organizing the brief is an activity which gives rise to thoughts of these proto-forms. Clearly, drawing is a crucial activity in Herman Hertzberger's process, but he sees this as a very different kind of drawing to that done by an artist, and is concerned that design drawings should not be seen as an end in themselves.[6]

A very crucial question is whether the pencil works after the brain or before. In fact what should be is that you have an idea, you think and then you score by means of words or drawing what you think. But it could also be the other way round, that while drawing, your pencil, your hand is finding something, but I think that's a dangerous way. It's good for an artist but it's nonsense for an architect.[7]

Of course, Herman Hertzberger recognizes the importance of the designer interacting with a drawing. 'You are influenced by what you are doing ... and sometimes inspired by a drawing ... but don't let the pencil determine your thoughts, it must be the other way round.'

Herman Hertzberger warns that designers often put too much reliance on the ability of their drawings to represent the reality of their designs. 'In no way do graphical representations or drawings represent more than themselves, and in no way can they represent space.' He is worried that some architects can become seduced by the quality of their own drawings, and can become blind to the inadequacies of their designs. 'Their drawings are beautiful and they sell well, but their buildings are disappointing.'

However, for Herman Hertzberger the very act of drawing remains a vital and integral part of his process, about which he now feels happy. 'It took me 40 years to find a way to have this communication of my brain and my paper ... and I feel I'm now quite eloquent in my way of doing it.' He is therefore not enthusiastic about computer-aided design since he feels no need to acquire the new skills necessary to use it rather than because he has any fundamental objection. 'I need all my energy for my design, and I decided [not to learn to use CAD] like I decided not to learn the violin at my age.'[8]

Herman Hertzberger talks with great passion about the users of his buildings and has rightly acquired an international reputation for this aspect of his work. He finds buildings that separate clients from users intrinsically more interesting to design:

I prefer, for instance, to make a school over making a house, because the house I feel has too much of a constraint to just follow the particularity and idiosyncrasy of just one person or a couple. I prefer to have a school where you have a board, you have teachers, you have parents and you have the children, and the users are all of them.[9]

[6] **Drawing**
This is a rather more subtle argument than there is space for here, and other authors have written extensively on the role of drawing in the design process. However, Herman Hertzberger is really directing our attention to the 'image trap' in which designers design their drawings rather than the buildings they are intended to represent.

[7] **Design and art**
There are two ways of interpreting the implicit views in this statement. First, there is the view that designing and creating art are recognizably different activities. This, of course, raises considerable philosophical problems, since design usually has artistic values and intentions. However, I have argued in *How Designers Think* that the source of design constraints as including clients, users and legislators together with the need for designed objects to be practically useful (i.e. radical constraints) differentiates design from art. The second way of interpreting Herman Hertzberger's statement here is simply that design drawings are not art, leaving open the question of whether or not the end product of design is art.

[8] **Computer-aided design**
This is an unusually moderate view about CAD. Most designers seem to feel strongly about CAD whether those views are positive or negative. However, it also represents a pragmatic view about skill. If that skill is highly developed and seems to serve you well, then perhaps it is best not to disturb it.

[9] **Client constraints and user constraints**
There can be little doubt that user constraints form the most potent primary generator for Herman Hertzberger.

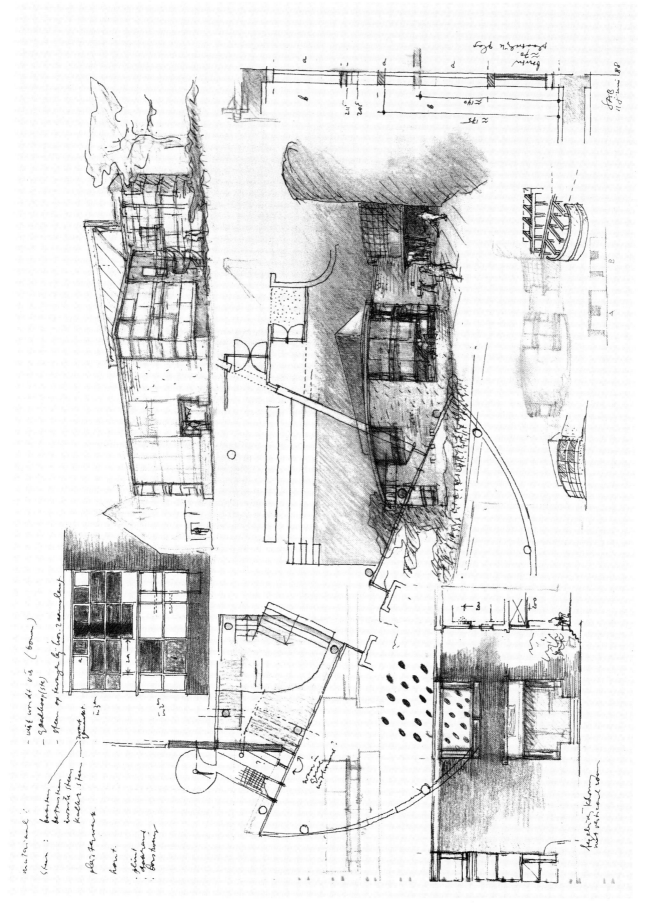

This study for a primary school is typical of Herman Herzberger's sketchbook. The combination and overlaying of plans, sections and perspective sketches is characteristic of his method.

Herman Hertzberger seems much less interested in formal methods of user participation than might be imagined from an examination of his work and his reputation.[10] 'I am just interested in seeing and listening, I don't need to talk with them [users], well, sometimes you have some questions but most of the thing is observation.' He argues strongly that architects are inadequately trained in the process of observation and believes they need to acquire the skills of the detective. 'That's why I am so fond of crime stories on television … where the detective, this person who uses his eyes, and he is not asking so many questions but he sees what happens.' This theme is taken up extensively in Herman Hertzberger's book, 'Lessons for Students of Architecture', in which he encourages the reader to observe behaviour in relation to the built environment. 'I happen to be inspired by the daily life going on.'

Although Herman Hertzberger 'loves doing competitions' and he does work on them when invited, he finds them frustrating due to the lack of contact with users and clients. 'I'm always lost at competitions, because you get a programme, sometimes stupid, sometimes very intelligent, and you do it, you have nice ideas … but nobody understands you, you have no communication.'

Herman Hertzberger also sees the relationship between designer and client as of critical importance in the design process.[11] He feels that for any real progress to made there must be what he refers to as a 'human relationship' which builds a fundamental level of trust between the two parties:

If you have not got a good relationship in the human sense with your client, forget it because they'll never trust you. They trust you as long as they have seen things they have eaten before, but as soon as you offer them a dish they have not eaten before you can forget it.

Herman Hertzberger returns to his theme of the unreliable interpretation of drawings again when discussing the client relationship. He also sees the client's reactions to his drawings as part of the communication process between client and designer:

A drawing without explanation is nothing, … clients always ask you to send a drawing one week before [a meeting] so they can study it, and I always try to find a pretext for not doing that, because I want to present them myself and open the drawings and look at their eyes to see what their first reaction is and to try to detect what the hard points are, and then trying to listen to their first question.

Herman Hertzberger clearly likes to discuss the emerging design with his clients and users throughout the process, but he also describes the reluctance that he feels to show design drawings to clients and users before he feels confident about them. For this reason he chooses to 'ask questions not in terms of form, but asking them a different way and in a different language'. He describes how he had the idea for a stepped section for one of the Apollo Schools and drew the idea on the blackboard in the school in order to get the client's reaction first-hand. He uses a similarly provocative approach when consulting specialists.[12]

I do not ask them 'How much ceiling space do you need for your pipes', I say 'Well, you get 15 cm. Is that OK?' And you get 'No, no, no, that's not OK, I need. . .' and then you really know.''

[10]**Guiding principles**
It is interesting that many of the user issues about which Herman Hertzberger talks are often not concerned with the primary function of the building. He is, as he says himself, 'inspired by daily life', and remains perhaps more interested in the social and personal life of the office worker than their function within the office organization. Perhaps this is reflected in the observational and anecdotal way in which he gathers his information in preference to formal participatory techniques. This might be contrasted with Richard Burton's use of formal techniques from social science.

[11]**The client**
Like so many of the designers in this book, Herman Hertzberger values his interaction with clients not just during brief making but throughout the design process. The question of the trust needed between designer and client is another popular theme echoed throughout this book, particularly by Eva Jiricna, Ian Ritchie and Denise Scott Brown and Robert Venturi.

[12]**Role of consultants**
This lesson would probably be a hard one to learn for many architects who seem to feel themselves in some way intellectually apart from technical consultants. Perhaps his provocative approach is allowed by Herman Hertzberger's consultants precisely because he also tries to make a positive response to their ideas. If so, this is rather a clever piece of social interaction, allowing him to push co-operative tension to its creative limits. John Outram seems to reflect a similar attitude to the creative involvement of consultants.

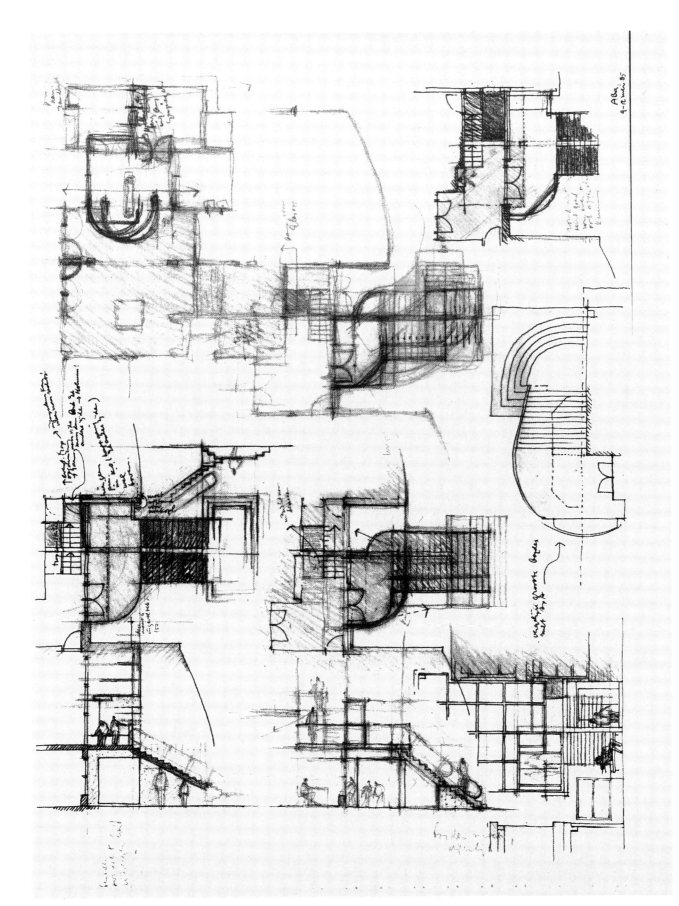

A single page from Herman Hertzberger's sketchbook, showing extraordinarily careful attention to the design of entrances, which offers a good example of his approach to architecture.

He thinks it very important to stimulate his consultants so that they become as enthusiastic as himself about the project.

When they come with proposals I never throw them out, even if their proposals are to me absolutely crazy or impossible or against my line of thinking, I still try to get something out of them.

Herman Hertzberger likes to describe and understand design problems, and believes in separating this process from that of finding solutions:

It seems to be very difficult not to mix up the questions 'What is the problem and what is the solution to the problem?' People have somewhere in their brains the idea that this must be done at once, which is not true.

He appreciates that these two processes of identifying problems and generating solutions must be linked, and likens this to a footballer receiving the ball and first controlling it before making his pass. 'Sometimes you are in the situation where you must direct it with one touch, but most of the time when you are not under this stress you first stop the ball.'[13]

The detail with which Hertzberger analyses problems is impressive and the comprehensiveness with which he finds problems shows the application of both creativity and enormous experience. His own description of the problem surrounding the design of the entrance stairs to one of his Apollo Schools in Amsterdam illustrates the point:

The problem is that you have certain moments when many children have to [pass through], the problem also is that sometimes you have a small number of people waiting, the problem is that sometimes it rains and then it is not very nice to sit there. the problem is ... and so on. So you get this whole list of things that altogether represent the problem. And then you say, well, given all these things, the stair should not be too small, should not be too large, it should be covered over, it should not be ... and so on. There are always these contradictions. This for me is creativity, you know, finding solutions for all these things that are contrary, and the wrong type of creativity is that you just forget about the fact that sometimes it rains, you forget that sometimes there are many people, and you just make beautiful stairs from the one idea you have in your head. This is not real creativity, it is fake creativity![14]

Just as he is critical of the 'fake' creativity so Herman Hertzberger disapproves of architecture which is generated purely from a consideration of external appearance. 'I detest solutions that are just based on external beauty and conceal, or better to say, deny the truth.' He readily admits that his own architecture often employs a characteristic set of materials, but he argues this frees him to concentrate on what he sees as the more important issues in the design process:

Well, I work a little bit like an artist who has only two or three colours on his palette, this is not laziness but is a sort of strategy not to distract with too many things ... there is so much to be hidden by the use of different materials because then you emphasize the graphical ... I do not dislike it but all too often it hides a lack of plasticity, a lack of space, and for me space for people is the thing.[15]

While trying to give his work layers of meaning, Herman Hertzberger does not believe in the use of symbolism as a major generating force. 'Too many architects escape into philosophical things in order to escape from

[13]**Finding problems**
Herman Hertzberger refers to the paradox that good designers seem to think in terms of three-dimensional solutions throughout the process, but also seem capable of delaying their attachment to any solution before fully understanding the problem. This relationship between finding problems and solving them seems to be one of the most difficult and critical parts of the design process.

[14]**Originality**
Herman Hertzberger seems to be drawing a distinction between originality and creativity, which are often confused by design critics. A solution may, of course, be original and even contribute substantially to our appreciation of some aspect of design, and yet may fail comprehensively to solve the problem for which it was a proposition. This confusion is all too easily generated in schools of design when tutors, wishing to applaud a student for original and imaginative work, condone functional inadequacies. This is possibly because tutors realize that the importance of solving that specific problem is small compared to the value of developing creativity. However, such slack criticism can lead to the encouragement of what Herman Hertzberger calls 'false creativity'. Robert Venturi makes a similar point with his comment that 'it is better to be good than to be original'.

[15]**Materials**
It is worth comparing this position with that of Eva Jiricna, who places great emphasis on the role of decisions about materials in her process. Herman Hertzberger's work does seem to use a fairly restricted range of materials, and he explains that this is not that he is disinterested in them, but that he is more interested in form. This raises an interesting question about the mental capacity of designers. Perhaps it is not possible to be innovative in every aspect of design simultaneously, and thus Herman Hertzberger is choosing to husband his intellectual resources carefully.

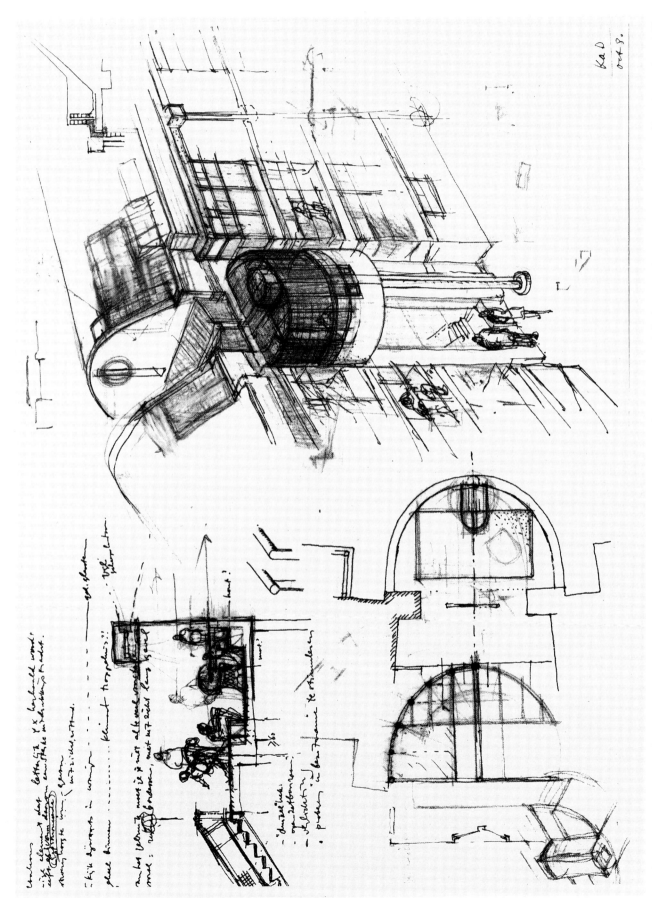

Herman Hertzberger has always been associated with a humanistic approach to architecture. This page from his sketchbook for housing at Kassel gives some indication of how this is achieved. The questions of view and privacy together with the ability of the users to control these elements were clearly central to the thinking behind this page.

doing the homework.' Although he has himself a very well developed and consistent philosophy based on structuralism running throughout his work, he does not believe that people should have to understand a philosophical position in order fully to appreciate architecture. In fact he believes designers, like architects, should be careful to explain their designs and the reasons behind them. 'Architects should learn to be explicit about their means and their objectives.' He dismisses the argument that this can be too difficult. He married a kindergarten teacher and draws a parallel with the need to explain difficult concepts to children. He uses a possibly apocryphal tale concerning a children's concert of Beethoven and Mozart. The introducer explained to the children that in listening to Beethoven they would hear the music of a man struggling to reach heaven, but in the music of Mozart they would hear the music of a man coming from heaven.[16] This rather impish story perhaps represents one of Herman Hertzberger's own most charming traits. He uses a sophisticated philosophical approach to grapple with some of the most complex and intractable problems on behalf of the users of his buildings, and yet he strives to give them understandable architecture that they can control for themselves.

[16]**Explaining design**
This might be contrasted with the story in which Wagner is said to have replied to a critic asking for an explanation of *The Ring*, that 'it is the explanation'. It often seems to be the case that designers are much less fluent with words than with form and space, and their explanations are often disappointing.

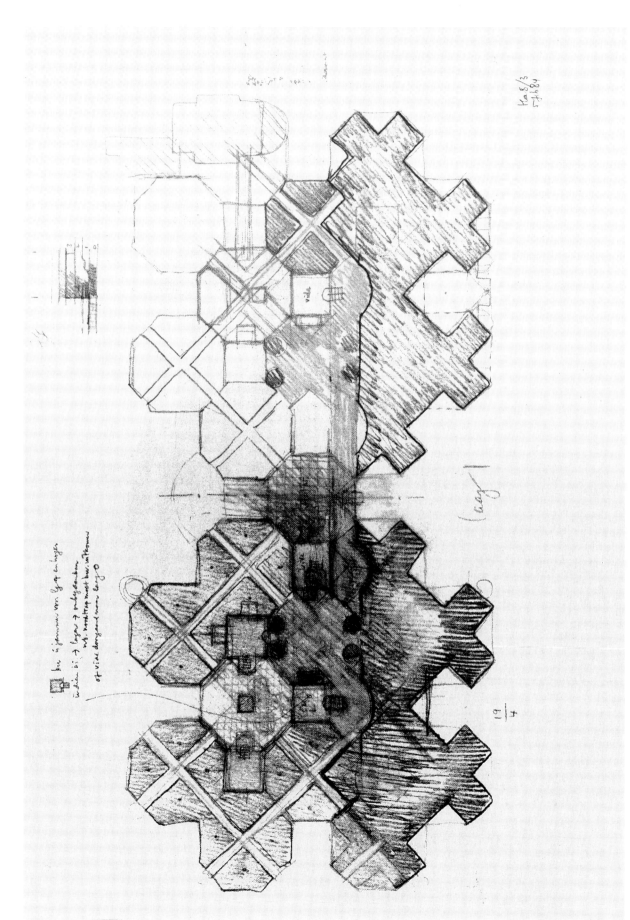

A sketch plan for the Ministry of Social Welfare and Employment in the Hague shows a continuation of the line of thought which was famously started in the Central Beheer office in Appledoorn.

Herman Hertzberger
Bibliography

Buchanan, P. (1985). Last resort: old people's home Almere. *Architectural Review*, **177**(1058), 27–35.

Buchanan, P. (1987). Beyond Beheer. *Architectural Review*, **181**(1083), 34–40.

Buchanan, P. (1990). Forum Fellowship. *Architectural Review*, **187**(1116), 30–71.

Duffy, F. (1988). Hertzberger on the slow track. *Architects' Journal*, 13 January, 36–41.

Hertzberger, H. (1963). Flexibility and polivancy. *Ekistics*, April, 238–239.

Hertzberger, H. (1980). Shaping the environment. In B. Mikellides (ed.), *Architecture for People* (pp. 38–40), London: Studio Vista.

Hertzberger, H. (1991). *Lessons for Students in Architecture* (Ina Rike, translator). Rotterdam: Uitgeverij 010.

van Tuyl, G. (ed.). (1990). *Herman Hertzberger: recent works 1980–1990*, The Hague: Rijksdienst Beeldende Kunst.

Weston, R. (1987). A question for Herman. *Architects' Journal* **186**(48), 24–26.

Woolley, T. (1989). Herman Hertzberger: the architecture of optimism. *Architecture Today*, **1**, 24–27.

Eva Jiricna

Eva Jiricna was born in the Czechoslovakian town of Zlin which became the centre of the empire built by Tomas Bata, who provided both factories and housing for the workers in his shoe business. This somewhat futuristic city, with its regular grids and modern buildings, must have made a considerable impact on the young Eva, particularly since her father, Josef Jiricny, was an architect for the Bata organization. Eva Jiricna describes him as 'very technically oriented, making his own radios and televisions', while her mother, by comparison, was 'interested in languages and literature and had absolutely no interest in anything of a technical nature, she thought it was all a great deal of a nuisance'. Eva Jiricna's own education had a very engineering bias; a choice she made herself 'because I wanted to avoid designing interiors, and being a girl, everybody was telling me I should do interiors'. In spite of her father's discouragement she went to university in Prague to study architecture. She graduated in 1962 and found her early career directed by the socialist state. However, she never joined the Communist Party and, after attending a UIA conference in Paris, Eva Jiricna resolved to cross the 'iron curtain' more permanently. This was later arranged in 1968 by Jack Whittle, who was working at the GLC Architects' Department. She stills uses the word 'freedom' in a manner which suggests that she regards it as more precious than those who have known nothing else.

She initially joined the GLC Architects' Department for a year before moving to Louis de Soissons to work on the Brighton Marina where, she claims, 'she was a nuisance to everybody when fussing about detail', and where she was to learn a great deal about materials. She left in 1978 to start a series of practices cooperating with others, including Jan Kaplicky of Future Systems, and with Richard Rogers on the interior of the Lloyd's building. In the early 1980s she established her long-running close association with Joseph Ettedgui for whom she has designed her well-known series of high-quality interiors. The 'Joseph' shops and the associated café were followed by fashion stores for other clients, night-clubs, and domestic interiors. After previous partnerships with David Hodges and the interior designer Kathy Kerr, Eva Jiricna Architects was founded in its current form in 1986.

Eva Jiricna describes herself as a person who just loves being organized but feels a constant failure in this respect. This typically self-deprecating remark conceals as much truth as it reveals. It would perhaps be accurate to describe Eva Jiricna's methodology, like her work, as a most unusual combination of the apparently logical and the astonishingly original. The closer the examination of her work and working method, the more paradoxical contrasts seem to prevail. She constantly talks of logical processes and yet produces the most original and distinctive environments. She applies an engineering background to the design not just of buildings but of interiors and uses the hardest and most high-technology materials as a setting for the most delicate of women's fashion. Eva Jiricna expresses a lack of interest in fashion and yet dresses with a distinctive style. She denies an interest in the symbolic values of her work and yet creates strong and lasting images.

The office itself echoes many of these essential and paradoxical characteristics of the practice. There is much evidence of method in the carefully organized library, high-tech furniture, and considerable use of black and neutral tones. Even the location near one of London's most fashionable shopping streets reflects the practice's most well-known work. Eva Jiricna has one associate upon whom she relies to take care of 'office administration and everything a small practice has to be burdened with'. There are between 12 and 14 staff in the practice, which is about the size she would like to see it. They handle between 10 and 15 jobs at any one time. She does not run any jobs herself but tries to keep in touch with all of them.[1]

Eva Jiricna is particularly concerned to ensure coordination in the work of each design team, describing the problem as making 'it look like it was all done by the same pair of hands'. She does not claim sole responsibility for this because, as she says, 'it's a question of the ability of your brain to store just so much information', but she does 'try to know about everything that goes on in every job'. Again characteristically modestly, she describes her special contribution in terms of 'being the oldest I am more aware of possible mistakes'.

When not dealing with clients or out on-site Eva Jiricna sits at a table with a sketch-pad rather than at her own drawing board.[2] 'If I am in the office most of my day then the time is spent with people sketching and sometimes we have got an engineer and sometimes another consultant and we just make scribbles and sketches and try to get it right.' Members of the practice come to Eva Jiricna's table to discuss their work and this interaction seems to be operated more by staff than by Eva Jiricna herself:

There are some people who come to me five times a day, and some people I only see once a week. It depends on their ability, on the project and it also depends on how capable people feel of handling something on their own.[3]

Eva Jiricna is quite definite in her view that the most important part of designing is finding rather than solving problems:

The design process is finding the questions; there is always an answer to every question. You have to find the questions and not the answers; then it's only a matter of time to find the answers, but the question is the difficult part.[4]

[1] Office size and structure
As with many other designers in this book, Eva Jiricna clearly has a view about how large she wishes the practice to be. The rest of the chapter will make it clear that its size is clearly limited by her approach, which is certainly more valued by her than purely expanding her practice. It should be remembered that a job in this office which specializes in interior design is probably very much smaller than projects in one of the larger practices in this book. However, the detail with which projects are carried out here probably makes each job rather more complex than might be assumed purely from the scale of work.

[2] Drawing
Ian Ritchie carries a small sketch-book around the office with him and Herman Hertzberger only draws on an A3 pad, which is a size also preferred by Santiago Calatrava and Michael Wilford. The idea that designers sit at large drawing boards is thus rather misleading. Several of the designers in this book have a distinct preference for working on small drawings.

[3] Intervention
Michael Wilford portrays himself as an editor waiting for 'copy' to come forward from his staff. Eva Jiricna seems to operate in a similar way. Even though they may be internationally known names, some designers seem to get the best results by giving a great deal of the initiative to their staff. Often the interaction is quite short and infrequent, as seen here. Herman Hertzberger similarly talks of only brief conversations to support a continual exchange of small drawings. The idea of sitting in the middle of the office rather than in a separate room is also shared with Ian Ritchie.

[4] Finding problems
This is a very similar view to that expressed by Herman Hertzberger. Although we tend to admire designers for their solutions, it is often their ability to find the right problems which distinguishes good from adequate or poor design.

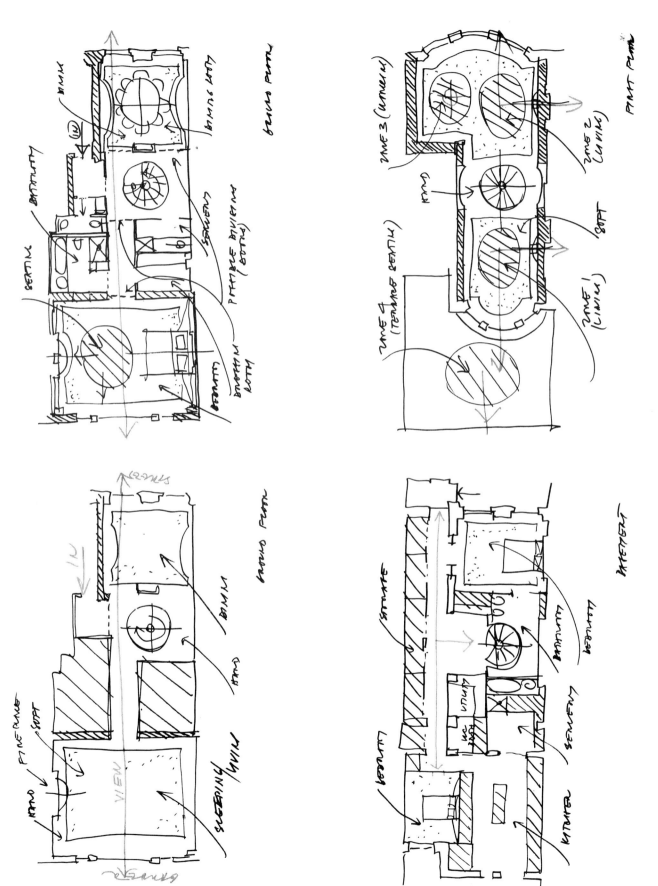

Two studies of the floor plan and one of both the basement and first floor for a house in London's Knightsbridge by Eva Jiricna.

She believes that design is a generic process: 'There is no difference between designing a teaspoon and designing a building in principle, it is the same approach, it requires the same skill.'[5] However, she also points out that each job is unique and thus requires its own special design process to evolve in response to the problem. 'Every time you start a new job it's a completely new story, and each story evolves slightly differently like the design process.' This view of the difference between jobs is perhaps particularly surprising in Eva Jiricna's case since she has worked so frequently for the same client. Perhaps this attitude is one of the reasons for the freshness of her work even though she has worked on many projects with apparently similar briefs.

Eva Jiricna talks of a story emerging as the design process proceeds which she clearly sees as having a logical development. 'When we do a new job we really go through exactly the same process, trying to identify the brief, trying to analyse what we are doing, and to find some kind of a logical basis which will give us a starting point to develop a story.' This illustrates another of the paradoxes associated with Eva Jiricna. She strongly believes that the basic design process is common not only across problems within architecture and interior design but also across traditional design disciplines such as industrial and product design. However, this should not be taken to imply a rigidity of approach since she is also convinced that each job is different, and becomes more so as the process develops. The process is thus seen as a response to the problem as much as a way of tackling it, and every problem is considered to be unique. 'There is never a job that would be completely identical to the previous one or even vaguely similar, so we always start from scratch.'

For Eva Jiricna the design process begins with a period of establishing the brief. While regarding clients as very important participants in the design process, Eva Jiricna also feels that briefing has to be done interactively:

We never, ever get a brief from the client which we can start working on.[6] *The client hardly ever knows exactly what they want, and sometimes they have got totally rigid ideas about what they want, but they are completely wrong, and they don't realize it.*

The involvement of the client is seen as central to the success of the process:

The worst client is the person who tells you 'get on with it and give me the final product'. This really doesn't work because first of all we don't know enough about the project. The client is not capable of knowing what the options are and we are not capable of understanding what the end product is for.[7]

Perhaps one of the most fascinating aspects of Eva Jiricna's design process is the way in which she manages the early phases.

When a project starts we always look at all the options we can think of and see which is the strongest and most appropriate one. I don't think it has ever happened that we would say 'that's it' straight away, there are always alternatives.

Eva Jiricna maintains that they always try to map out what she calls all the basic alternatives, perhaps up to ten initially. These alternatives all get worked up together until they fail for some reason or other:

[5]Design as a generic process
This view is commonly asserted in early design methodology literature, although it is interesting to note that most of its proponents were engineers.

[6]The brief
This view that a design brief is rarely (if ever) a comprehensive description of the problem is expressed by many designers in this book. Several, including Herman Hertzberger and Michael Wilford, seem to like to start with extremely short briefs. This leads on to the view that the brief is most satisfactorily developed as an interactive process between client and designer. The nature of the brief and how to develop it seem to be poorly understood by many clients.

[7]The client
Virtually all the designers in this book emphasize the importance of the role of the client in the design process. This is probably one of the most succinctly argued reasons why that might be so.

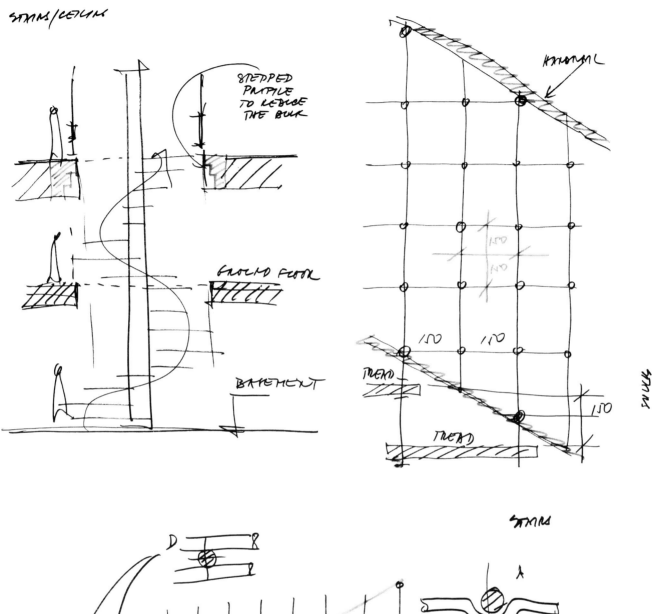

Studies of the central and focal staircase which connects the three floors of the Knightsbridge house.

On the first morning when you start working on the scheme you have got, let's say, ten and they are all equally possible and then you go through a process of analysing it and develop each of them slightly further on, and then you are left with, say, five. That process goes on and eventually you are left with one alternative.[8]

This idea of mapping out the range of alternatives could perhaps be seen to come from Eva Jiricna's engineering-oriented education, where such a technique might be more conventional. At first it seems difficult to imagine an interior designer working in such an open-ended situation trying to map out alternatives. However, this becomes much more understandable once one appreciates how these alternatives are selected.

For Eva Jiricna a key early decision is almost invariably about materials. She thinks that 'in a way material dictates the concept ... and materials are not interchangeable ... to me the material really is the starting point of the story'. The linguistic references continue in her argument here because she believes that 'each material has its own language and every time you use it, you learn just one more word, one more expression, a little bit of grammar'. This in turn raises another item on Eva Jiricna's agenda; that of minimizing the number of materials used. She argues that since each material has its own language then too many materials will result in an incoherent scheme.[9]

The choice of materials is also a logical process for Eva Jiricna, very much related to the developing brief. 'For example if we know it is a public building, we ask what is durable? What materials will survive in a specific environment?' She recognizes, of course, that cost comes into this early decision, and also what the client will accept. 'We have some clients who wouldn't like to have stainless steel and are terrified of having metals anywhere in the environment.'

The next set of decisions in this process have to do with the way materials are fitted together, and Eva Jiricna draws full-size details even before general layouts:

In our office we usually start with full-size details ... if we have, for example, some ideas of what we are going to create with different junctions, then we can create a layout which would be good because certain materials only join in a certain way comfortably.

She accepts that this is a rather unusual approach. 'I think you will probably find this a completely heretic view because most of the people I have ever worked with start making little sketches.' Of course, the plan is not neglected, and Eva Jiricna talks of a 'parallel process' in which spatial concepts are explored.[10] However, she is very firm that 'we don't go from a concept which is based on, say, creating little boxes and so on, and then leave the details to the end'.

Eva Jiricna has already expressed her view that design is a matter of dividing the problem into smaller problems which can be solved more or less individually and then building the final design up by adding these solutions together:

Each big decision splits down into smaller design problems. You solve each of these in turn and you have your result.[11]

[8] Alternatives
Both Richard Burton and Michael Wilford clearly describe a process based on the generation of alternatives and then selecting from them, though neither use the particular method described here.

[9] Guiding principles
Eva Jiricna has a strong conviction that a design will emerge from the careful study of the nature of materials and methods of joining them. This is a excellent illustration of a set of general guiding principles being used as a way of generating a series of alternative primary generators. This particular focus on materials, however, seems almost unique to Eva Jiricna, although there are some similarities with Santiago Calatrava's way of working. She describes design as an entirely logical process of choosing between these alternatives, and in this regard sounds much in sympathy with Michael Wilford, although he would be more likely to base his alternatives on functional planning than materials.

[10] Parallel lines of thought
This is a good example of what seems to be a common characteristic of cognition in the design process. Several lines of thought are developed more or less in parallel, and in this case Eva is indicating that she thinks about the grammar of the details in the scheme in parallel with general spatial concepts. What seems to characterize good designers is their willingness to allow these lines of thought to remain parallel for some considerable time rather than forcing them to converge. Such designers seem quite content with the notion that these lines of thought may not appear to be reconcilable and yet are prepared to invest mental effort into them all. Clearly this is not as illogical or wasteful as it seems.

[11] Sub-dividing the problem
This sounds very much like the famous method of Christopher Alexander, which attracted much theoretical approval but without ever having been used as a practical technique.

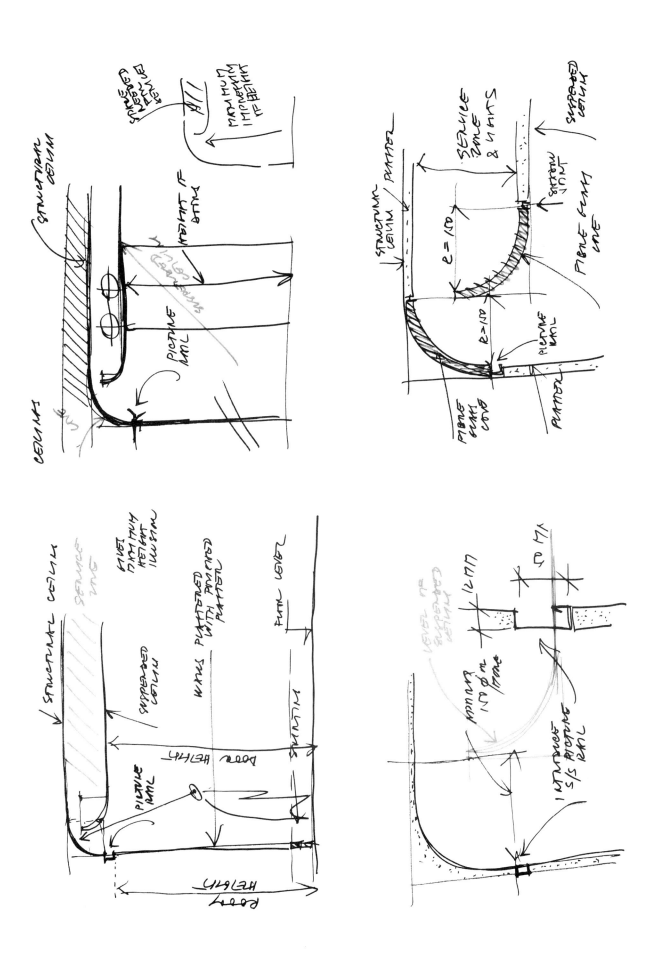

Eva Jiricna pays particular attention to the junctions between elements, as is demonstrated here by studies of the wall and ceiling junction.

In fact, these problems seem to be aspects of the problem rather than discrete elements or sub-problems, and clearly overlap, and are selected in order to handle the whole issue mentally:

It's an impossible task to design a building [as a whole], you have to split it up. First you might look at the site, you don't yet know the orientation of the building and you go through every single aspect and set little exercises, so first of all you know how the sun travels, you know where any water is, you know whether the site is flat, you know where people are coming from and you work out where would be the best place for them to enter the site and the building. So each programme just gets split into a series of individual tasks and it's just like little pieces of paper which you put on the table.

What links this idea of decomposing the problem to Eva Jiricna's key decision on materials is the idea of building up the solution from small elements:

You just can't put them all together like that, so you start building up. First of all, you establish a building system which is made of certain pieces and then you have to find a logical way of building them up into something which could be used as a final scheme which is coherent.

Thus it is possible to see how a choice of materials leads to decisions about junctions through full-size details which can in turn lead to a consideration of general layout and spatial assembly.[12]

The word 'logical' occurs frequently in Eva Jiricna's description of her design process. She has little time for obscure theory and abstract ideas, or the symbolic content of architecture:

It's not an abstract process. I think that if you are a painter or a sculptor then it's all very abstract but architecture is a very concrete job. I really think that all that philosophy is a false interpretation of what really happens. You get an idea, but that idea is not really of a very philosophical or conceptual thought. It is really something which is an expression on the level of your experience which is initiated by the question. I don't think that great buildings have got great symbolic thinking behind them. I leave it to journalists and architectural critics to find a deep symbolic meaning because I don't think that anybody who looks at buildings can actually read the thinking behind them, and to me it's just totally useless.[13]

Perhaps it is because Eva Jiricna has designed so many shops that she came to view architecture as providing a background for the users to inhabit and of which they can take possession:

Architects don't produce the final product, architects produce the background and far more things are going to happen in front of the background, activities, people, clothes, merchandise, books in libraries. You have to think about what other people want and what kind of control you will have when you leave the site, and what you leave to the other people.[14]

This thinking about what the users will do with her designs, for example, leads Eva Jiricna to design shops in a way which reflects how she thinks the client will arrange their 'foreground' objects.

[12]**Assembly of components**
This idea of building a kind of design lexicon with components which have rules of arrangement and attachment can also be seen in Herman Hertzberger's work although it is not discussed in detail here.

[13]**Symbolism**
This view is shared by Richard Burton and, to some extent, by Herman Hertzberger and Michael Wilford. By contrast, Ian Ritchie seems much more interested in an underlying philosophy, and the symbolic content of his work is clearly a design generator and John Outram seems to use symbolism as a major guiding principle.

[14]**Background**
Richard Burton similarly has this view that what the architect does is only a part of creating a place. He has worked to include art and activities within his buildings. Other designers seem almost obsessive in their wish to control the total environment, even down to the cutlery in the case of Arne Jacobsen.

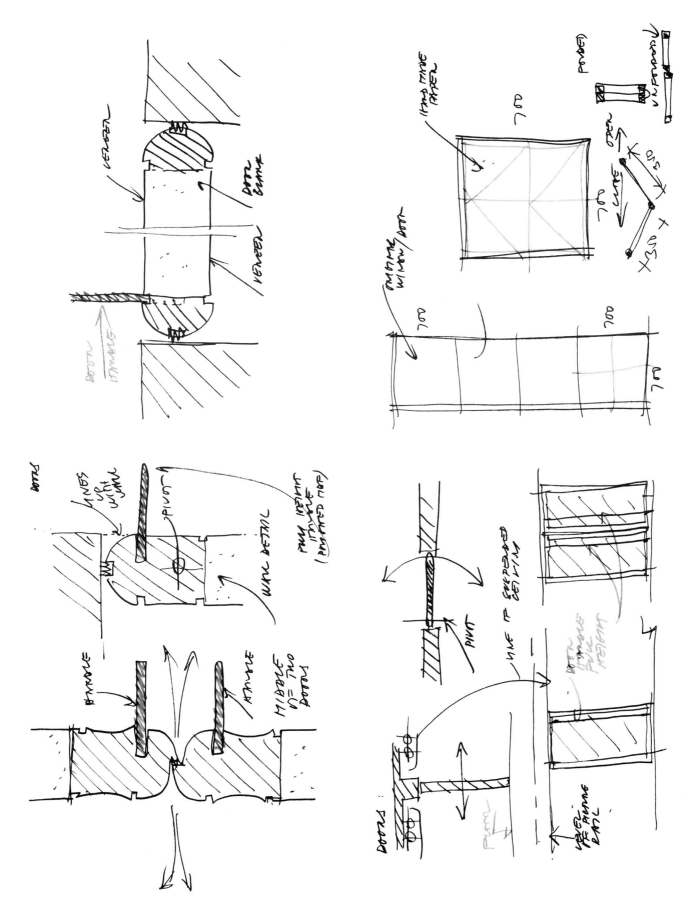

Sketches by Eva Jiricna of the detail and organization of dcors and windows in the Knightsbridge house.

With Kenzo you just make one rail because everything is so beautifully merchandized, but we did another shop in Florence for a lady who sells 22 different designers so we did little recesses in the wall.

Eva Jiricna has done most of her recent work for clients who will themselves be the users, but earlier in her career she worked for the GLC and others in situations more remote from the users of her buildings. She believes that designers can always find out about the users' needs if they are willing. However, she clearly prefers to work in a very close relationship with her clients. She expends considerable energy in establishing this relationship and nursing it through the job whilst maintaining her own objectives. She achieves this by bringing the client along using verbal agreement before drawing designs. 'I try to express in words what they want, and then I try to twist it into a different statement and then draw it.'[15] By this means Eva Jiricna has managed to design in entirely modern hi-tech materials even when the client initially expressed a wish for an early nineteenth-century restoration. She takes care, however, to educate her clients, explaining, for example, how a traditional cornice solved the problem of the wall/ceiling junction, and how this problem is different when a suspended ceiling is used, thus resulting in a contemporary resolution. The fact that so much of Eva Jiricna's work is a repeat for clients suggests that they are more than happy with this educative approach.[16]

Eva Jiricna is not sure that we shall ever come out of the current confusion of styles and movements in architecture. She argues that the freedom of modern society in terms of movement, communications, and political systems will maintain this pluralism, just as has happened in fashion. Although she is probably seen as an exponent of hi-tech, this is really rather misleading. In fact Eva Jiricna believes in design reflecting its time and she is implacably opposed to copying historical styles. But she is not, at heart, a stylist at all. She just happens to use materials and the way they work and must be fitted together as her most important design generator:

I just don't find that any forceful styling approach is the answer to anything. Everything has to come from a proper solid, logical background, but then it can go in any direction you like.[17]

Eva Jiricna would most certainly not agree that the plan is the generator, but she would probably feel that success is very much achieved in the details.

[15]**Relationship with the client**
This method of progressively reaching agreement with the client about the principles of a design before the appearance is revealed in drawings is similar to that employed by Michael Wilford, although he is working more with committee clients. In psychological terms it can be seen as a way of not only involving the client in the process but also committing them to feel some ownership of the solution.

[16]**Explaining design**
Herman Hertzberger also believes very strongly that designers should do more to explain the reasons behind their designs. It is interesting to note that Eva Jiricna and Herman Hertzberger have also both taught design.

[17]**Style**
Many of the designers in this book claim not to be interested in style, and many seem at times slightly resentful of the critics' attempts to categorize their work in this way. Critics, of course, concentrate on the end product of design rather than the process. Many designers seem to feel that if the way they worked were better understood these categories of style would become irrelevant.

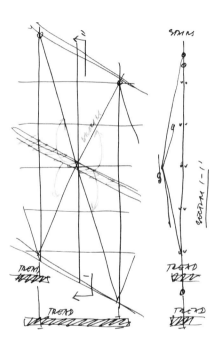

The upper floor of the Knightsbridge house showing the top of the central circular staircase, together with a sketch for the handrail construction. (photograph by Arcaid)

Eva Jiricna

Bibliography

Davey, P. (1989). Jiricna bravura. *Architectural Review*, **185**(1103), 36–40.

Gardner, C. (1991). Stairway to the stars. *RIBA Journal*, **98**(12), 45–47.

Lorenz, C. (1990). *Women in Architecture: a contemporary perspective*, New York: Rizzoli.

Manser, J. (1991). *The Joseph Shops*, London: Architecture Design and Technology Press.

Pawley, M. (1990). *Eva Jiricna: Design in Exile*, London: Fourth Estate.

Viladas, P. (1986). Lean not mean. *Progressive Architecture* (September 1986), 16–21.

Wilcock, R. (1987). All ship shape. *RIBA Journal*, **95**(11), 98–101.

Richard MacCormac

Richard MacCormac was born in 1938. He studied architecture at the University of Cambridge and at the Bartlett School in the University of London. At Cambridge he was heavily influenced by the work of both Leslie Martin and Lionel March and met his future partner Peter Jamieson. He admits to having an 'almost obsessive interest' in the Prairie Houses of Frank Lloyd Wright which he was awarded a travelling scholarship to study. He continues greatly to admire the work of Frank Lloyd Wright, but has since developed an almost equal respect for Sir John Soane. He set up his own small practice after qualifying in 1969, although the partnership with Peter Jamieson was formed soon after in 1972, and was eventually also to include David Prichard.

The practice quickly became known for a series of influential projects all largely at the domestic scale. These included a number of low-rise housing schemes including student accommodation as well as a number of academic university buildings at both Oxford and Cambridge.

Richard MacCormac has written and lectured extensively on his approach to architecture, and remains a popular speaker in schools of architecture. He has taught architecture at Cambridge and was appointed George Simpson Professor of Architecture at Edinburgh University in 1982 and has sat on a number of educational committees.

He was elected president of the Royal Institute of British Architects in 1991 and his term of office was marked by a consistent emphasis on the quality of design. He has warned of what he sees as the potential harm to the quality of design caused both by 'design and build' and by the British government's recent attitude towards competitive tendering for architects' fees. Richard MacCormac has campaigned to exhibit and explain architecture in a more publicly accessible manner in 'architecture centres'. The end of his presidency was celebrated by the 'Art of the Process' exhibition at the RIBA, which showed the evolution of designs by a series of well-known British architects.

The practice of MacCormac, Jamieson, Prichard has more normally had about 24 staff but has grown to nearly twice that size. Each project has its own design team with up to ten working on the largest projects in the office. The practice has tended to design buildings of a residential scale and has developed what Richard MacCormac describes as 'a sort of vernacular' approach to these projects. MacCormac does not use the word 'vernacular' so much to refer to the style and appearance of their architecture but rather to the process itself. 'We have established a kind of typological repertoire which is to do with density and the main problems like car parking and so on.'

Richard MacCormac himself has been combining his own practice with his term of office as President of the RIBA. He sees his role in the practice as 'to initiate the design process in all major jobs', but here he is particularly referring to those projects which do not fit into the 'vernacular' pattern. One of the other partners Peter Jamieson takes a 'technical and contractual role' looking after problems on-site and reviewing the designs technically. Another partner, David Prichard, is 'very much a job runner' and leads the design teams. Richard MacCormac feels that their organizational structure is not very clearly defined, something which he sees as an advantage.[1]

Richard MacCormac speaks about his role as 'making a series of interventions at different stages in the design process'. He likes to have a degree of detachment from the everyday running of the project which allows him to intervene at what he considers to be critical moments. 'Part of the game is to create a crisis by recognizing that something is not right.'[2] He describes how such a series of interventions work in relation to the practice's design for the new Headquarters and Training Building for Cable and Wireless:

At the very beginning of the process the centre of the scheme was a circular courtyard, but later I thought this was wrong. By then we had this V idea going in which the building opens in a V shape rather like the wings of a bird ... towards this wonderful landscape. Then suddenly I had this idea that the courtyard should be pulled into an oculus, a sort of eye shape which would reflect the dynamic of the whole project.

This reflects a central theme of Richard MacCormac's approach to design – the struggle to understand an emerging idea, and to recognize and describe it so that it may be may worked out and resolved. He describes how on the same project he and one of his assistants were working over the weekend on the residential section of the scheme:

I can't quite remember what happened and either Dorian or I said 'it's a wall, it's not just a lot of little houses, it's a great wall 200 metres long and three storeys high ... we'll make a high wall then we'll punch the residential elements through that wall as a series of glazed bays which come through and stand on legs ... .[3]

[1] Office size and structure

At its largest this practice would be a similar size to that of ABK. However, the structure is very different, employing a more corporate system of allocating responsibilities. This method of working where each partner plays a particular role presumably suited to their interests and strengths is different to the form of organization found in the other multipartner practices reviewed in this book. Stirling and Wilford both operate in parallel and Ahrends Burton and Koralek tend to operate almost as three practices. It is interesting to note that Denise Scott Brown and Robert Venturi have recently moved away from this kind of structure.

[2] Intervention

This conscious use of intervention to disturb or shake up the design process shows some similarities with the ideas expressed by Richard Burton. Clearly the timing and nature of Richard MacCormac's interventions in this way must be critical to their success. At the time of writing this book Richard MacCormac probably found himself rather more detached from the daily working of the design team than normal, since he was also President of the RIBA!

[3] Conceptualizing and the central idea

This idea of naming a concept occurred frequently in conversation with Richard MacCormac and can also be seen repeated in much of his writing. Most of the examples to be found here referred to geometrical forms such as oculus, pinwheel and pendentive, or to types of place such as belvedere and walled garden. It seems to be a device to better understand an emerging idea or design concept. Once named in this way, the designers can share all the implications inherent in the idea and work them out in order to test the appropriateness of the idea to this particular scheme. It also serves to keep the design team together, as it were, in ensemble. As Richard MacCormac puts it, 'the right connections must be made'. There are considerable similarities between what Richard MacCormac is saying here and the search for conceptual ideas expressed by Ian Ritchie.

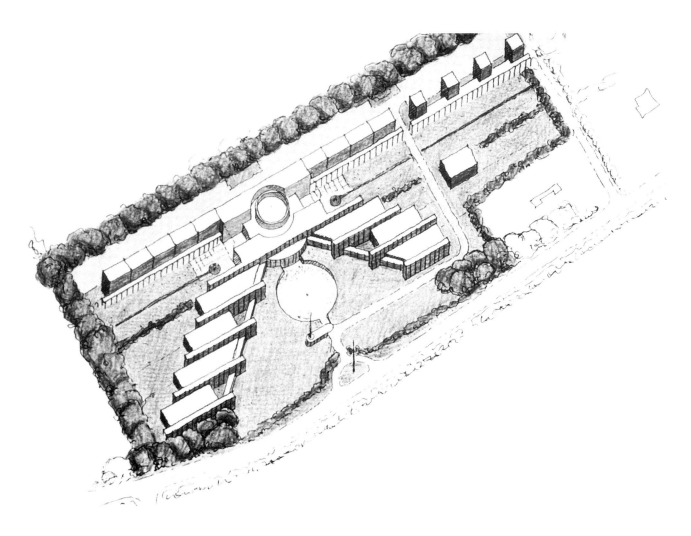

'At the very beginning of the process the centre of the scheme was a circular courtyard, but later I thought this was wrong. By then we has this 'V' idea going in which the building opens out in a 'V' shape rather like the wings of a bird . . . Then suddenly I had this idea that the courtyard should be pulled into an oculus, a sort of eye shape which would reflect the dymanic of the whole project . . .'

'I can't quite remember what happened and either Dorian or I said 'it's a wall, it's not just a lot of little houses, it's a great wall 200 metres long and three storeys high . . . we'll make a high wall then we'll punch the residential elements through that wall as a series of glazed bays which come through and stand on legs.'

(Richard MacCormac on the design process for the Headquarters and Training Building for Cable and Wireless.)

This design concept which emerged from one of Richard MacCormac's self-induced crises eventually revolutionized and organized the whole design. However, this can only be a team activity in Richard MacCormac's view:[4]

I or somebody else comes up with an originating idea, some idea that seems powerful enough to generate a scheme and to subsume a lot of decisions within it[5] ... it needs somebody in the team to pick up the ball and run with it. (Dowson and MacCormac, 1990). I find that I seize on somebody in the team who understands what the crisis is ... you have to find this person who sees what it is about otherwise it's hopeless.[6]

Richard MacCormac believes that architecture is what he calls 'a medium of thought' which is 'a kind of analogical or metaphorical way of thinking'. However, he is no abstract philosopher but rather a simultaneously passionate and yet practical man who sees 'the deeper structures of architectural thought as the means of reconciling the methodological and empathetic aspects of architecture'.

He is quite cynical about the traditional design brief. 'The real problem is often concealed by the way it is written about as a brief.' This attitude leads him to have mixed feelings about design competitions which, he admits, are simultaneously frustrating and exhilarating, but he worries that they can be 'rather hit and miss' because of the lack of contact between designer and client. 'Often in competitions the winning scheme is the one that tells the client something that they never knew before ... something that is terribly important to them and was not in the brief.'[7] He seems fascinated by the mystery of where design ideas originate and frequently refers to the struggle to understand an emerging design idea. 'Issues which are the stuff of the thing often only come out when you try and solve, when you try and produce a scheme, and therefore the design process defines objectives in a way in which the brief could never do.'

Richard MacCormac is convinced that design solutions and problems emerge together very much as reflections of each other. He clearly sees analysis and synthesis as closely intertwined processes which between them allow the architect to understand both brief and design concept. 'In our office we design as a means of coming to terms with the brief and recognize a reciprocal relationship between the production of form and the definition of the programme.' This notion of reciprocal functionalism forms one of the principal ideas informing Richard MacCormac's design process. He recognizes that 'although rooted in modern movement ... these concerns ... are a critique of the slogan "form follows function" and we believe that to some extent, the reverse is and should be true'.

He is fond of the journey as a metaphor for the design process, which he claims, like all art, is a reflection of life itself. 'The design process is a journey, an episodic journey towards a destination which you don't know about.' He speaks of the trials of this journey and the need to keep staff 'loyal to the process', and he recognizes the pain that designers suffer. Perhaps in part due to his tactic of creating crises, he openly admits that the journey can become 'terribly fraught ... with people literally in tears'. However, it is the 'big idea' that keeps designers going throughout a process which he believes is 'unsustainable unless it's very idealistic':

[4]The design team
It is very clear from listening to Richard MacCormac talking about the evolution of his designs that he genuinely cannot remember from which member of the design team each idea originates. Indeed, ideas are obviously not born in an instance but develop and clarify over time, with members of the design team contributing to that process. This indicates a very close, almost intimate, method of group working.

[5]Primary generator
This seems to be a fairly clear statement of the idea of a 'primary generator'. It can be seen as a strong organizing idea from which a substantial amount of the basic design concepts flow. Richard MacCormac seems to be telling us that once this idea exists, and is understood, then many decisions can be made almost automatically. Thus this represents a device for reducing uncertainty, a way of eliminating alternatives.

[6]The design team and the central idea
Richard MacCormac lays great emphasis on the need to have the whole design team understanding and sharing the concept behind the primary generator. This is a recognition of the obvious but often neglected fact that today design on this scale is a team rather than individual activity. This team, like those on the sports field, must 'play together' or 'be on the same wavelength'. A prerequisite for this to happen is the establishment of a sort of 'office culture' to which both Richard MacCormac and Sir Philip Dowson make reference in their discussion on Design Delegation, which contains this particular quotation.

[7]Design competitions
Richard MacCormac is known for his criticism of the way some clients use competitions as a means of exploiting designers without giving adequate reward. However, here he seems to be making a most important point which flows from much of what is said in this book about the nature of the design brief. Many of our designers have commented on the frustration of working on a competition without access to the client, and this seems to be strongly linked to the wish of these designers to involve the client in the design process itself, and consequently to see the initial brief as merely a starting point in what Richard MacCormac calls a journey of discovery about both problem and solution. What MacCormac is telling us here is that the competition can be quite a good vehicle through which the client may come to understand their problem better without necessarily establishing the working client/architect relationship. Perhaps a more public and explicit recognition of this role might result in a better use of the design competition.

The 'oculus' as developed in a later model.

This is not a sensible way of making a living, it's completely insane. There has to be this big thing that you're confident you're going to find. You don't know what it is you're looking for and you hang on.[8]

This emphasis on the idealistic nature of design and the search for a 'big idea' is also backed up by Richard MacCormac's practical side. He talks a great deal about the need to understand this idea and to follow it right through the detailed design stage. 'It's a matter of trying to find the life of the idea in the way it's detailed and made and that is incredibly difficult and hugely important really.' Richard MacCormac goes so far as to say that the detailed design stage is 'where architecture stands or falls'. He feels that the American term of 'design development' is therefore a more accurate description of this critical phase of design. Richard MacCormac talks of the need to maintain continuity between the conceptual stages and these detailed stages of design in order that the 'right connections are made'. This attitude leads him to be concerned about design and build packages which he feels can be disastrous.[9]

This argument can be seen very clearly in the development of MacCormac's acclaimed design for the chapel at Fitzwilliam College in Cambridge. Very early in the process an idea about playing round and square shapes together began to emerge. 'At some stage the thing became round but I can't quite remember how.' Eventually the upper floor began to float free of the structure supporting it. 'The congregational space became a sort of ship.' However, it was not until quite detailed problems were considered such as the resolution of balcony and staircase handrails that this idea was fully understood and the 'vessel' took on its final shape and relationship to supporting structure.

Richard MacCormac has no enthusiasm for technology as an end in itself or as a major driving force generating design ideas, although he admires the work of many 'hi-tech' architects:

The choices that we make about how we express construction are more to do with aesthetics than they are to do with the technological exigencies of the situation ... but I do share with the so-called hi-tech people a sense that what is worth doing is to clarify and make evident how a thing is put together and what its nature is.

If any consistent set of generators can be seen throughout Richard MacCormac's work it is those to do with basic geometry. There is a strong sense of organization about the work of the practice and this seems to be introduced at a very early stage in MacCormac's thinking about a scheme. He thinks that 'architects try to translate the stuff of briefs into some kind of structure as soon as possible'. In the early years of the practice these ideas were quite explicit and formal and were clearly the result of Richard MacCormac's time studying at Cambridge, where he was particularly influenced by the ideas of Sir Leslie Martin and Lionel March:[10]

We look for a clear geometric analogy for the content of the problem. All our schemes have a geometric basis, whether it is the pinwheel arrangement of Westoning, the courtyard system of Coffee Hall flats and Robinson College, the specific tartan grid of the Blackheath houses or the circle-based geometry of Hyde Park Gate. (MacCormac & Jamieson, 1977).

More recently the geometry is becoming more relaxed and informal but it remains a strong generator of design ideas. Richard MacCormac describes

[8]Sense of purpose
This point is also made very strongly by Ian Ritchie. Quite simply, the business of bringing a design idea to realization, particularly in the form of a building, requires a huge amount of determination, patience and perhaps stubborn doggedness. What both Richard MacCormac and Ian Ritchie are telling us is that it is the dedication to the deep underlying ideas behind the design that feeds this process and sustains the designer throughout this long and painful task.

[9]Continuity
Richard MacCormac raises this issue frequently in his writing and public speeches. He believes that we must be extremely careful to protect the 'environment of design' to ensure high quality. In particular, he is concerned that unless there is continuity from the earliest phases of design right through design development to detailed design, those important underlying ideas will get lost. All too often books on the design process tend to deal much more with the glamorous early conceptual phases of design, but Richard MacCormac is reminding us of the importance of the detailed phases. How could the continuity of ideas which Richard MacCormac calls for be maintained through a design and build procurement system?

[10]Guiding principles
Richard MacCormac clearly brings a continuing interest in geometrical systems into each design process with him. In this sense therefore we can see this as a designer-generated constraint of a formal kind. Since this seems to be a recurring theme in MacCormac's work, and because he has also written about it, we can interpret it as a set of guiding principles. The geometrical devices which result from this in the form of grids and forms become primary generators which structure the problem and solution. However, see also the next note for an elaboration of this idea.

The 'great wall' as developed in a later model.

in detail how their scheme for the Bristol University Faculty of Arts was based on what he calls a 'grid of relationships'. This scheme required the adaptation of a row of existing houses with new accommodation linking them to the rear. The solution incorporates strong geometrical rules even though these use irregular shapes partly derived from the existing Victorian houses and their garden boundaries. This more flexible geometry allows for a range of definitions of territorial arrangements from the individual department up to the shared faculty space. 'We saw the design problem as one of discovering an organizational analogy between the brief and what existed.'(MacCormac, 1983).

This illustrates an interesting principle behind Richard MacCormac's attitude towards geometry. He has studied the geometry of architecture in its own right and his thinking and conversation are littered with references to organizing devices such as grids and structures, and to forms such as domes and pendentives. However, in MacCormac's mind these always remain subservient to a greater purpose. 'Geometry is used as a means of making distinctions between one kind of place and another so that different activities take place in situations which have their own identity and, through use, can increase their distinctiveness' (MacCormac and Jamieson, 1977). At Bristol it was the definition of faculty and departmental territory, and in much of the housing it is the organization of family and group territories. 'The motive and incentive, as distinct from the method for this housing work, has been social.' In his often-expressed admiration for the work of Sir John Soane, Richard MacCormac lays great emphasis of the ability of the geometry of architecture to create an environment of light and shade. He describes how his practice makes use of a 'repertoire of tricks' which draw significantly on his study of Soane's work (MacCormac, 1985).[11]

Another lesson which Richard MacCormac has learnt from his study of Soane is that of the importance of drawing. 'All Soane's projects involved an enormous amount of drawing ... That process is a fundamental reminder to architects of the thinking pencil' (MacCormac, 1985). MacCormac himself admits to feeling incomplete as a thinker unless he has a pencil in his hand. 'Whenever we have a design session or a crit review session in the office I cannot say anything until I've got a pencil in my hand ... I feel the pencil to be my spokesman, as it were.' What is perhaps surprising coming from such a geometrically creative and innovative designer is the admission of just how dependent he is on the act of drawing. 'I haven't got an imagination that can tell me what I've got without drawing it ... I use drawing as a process of criticism and discovery.'[12] This leads Richard MacCormac to question whether computer-aided design can ever really replace this process of drawing as a thinking tool. However, he also sees dangers in allowing the drawing process to dominate the designer's thoughts. He recently organized a weekend urban design workshop on London and found himself working on areas of Bermondsey. 'I was drawing whole chunks of Bermondsey without any feeling for it at all, the felt tip was drawing things that I didn't like at all, it was being a felt-tip pen and not a piece of Bermondsey.'[13]

[11]**Intentions and mechanisms**
This seems to be a fundamentally important point that Richard MacCormac is making here which we might use to refine the concept of the primary generator. Although MacCormac's work seems littered with examples of formal constraints as primary organizing ideas, he is suggesting that these geometrical devices are in reality merely mechanisms through which a greater purpose is realized. What we see here therefore is the experience of the designer in knowing how such geometrical devices work and the effects they produce. This might be likened to a composer knowing how certain musical keys and key changes create moods. It reveals the necessity for designers to study these devices in their own right in order to establish their own vocabulary or 'repertoire of tricks', which may then be applied to express the greater ideas behind each design.

[12]**Drawing**
It is interesting to note how many of our designers are apparently quite humble about their own ability to imagine three-dimensional form and space without drawing it. See particularly Richard Burton, Herman Hertzberger and Eva Jiricna's comments about this. Richard MacCormac agrees very much with Donald Schon's delightful image of the designer having a conversation with his drawing, which is also referred to by Denise Scott Brown. There seems a general consensus that the act of drawing during the design process is indeed an extremely reflective one in which the designer 'talks to himself' through the pencil. The idea that it is difficult to think and talk about design matters without holding the pencil is commonly expressed by designers. Just as it is sometimes necessary to 'think aloud'.

[13]**Drawing**
Richard MacCormac is expressing a concern here similar to that voiced by Herman Hertzberger and Ian Ritchie. Essentially, this is the danger of the power of design drawings to take over and lead their own life such that the designer tends to design the drawing and not the real object. This is a tendency common among design students.

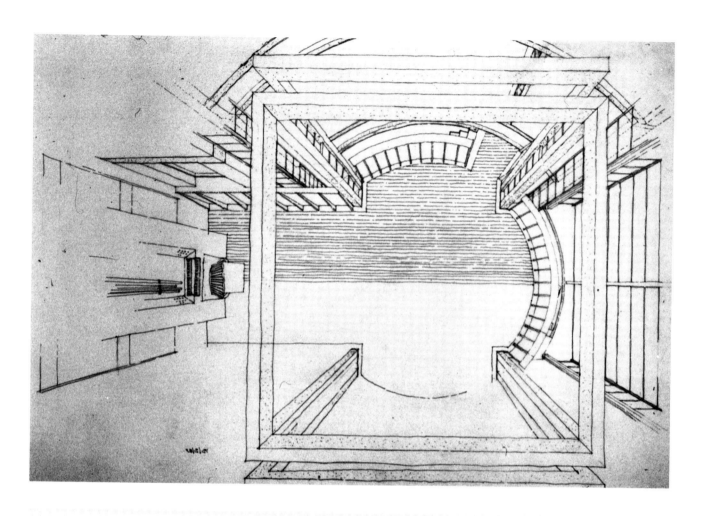

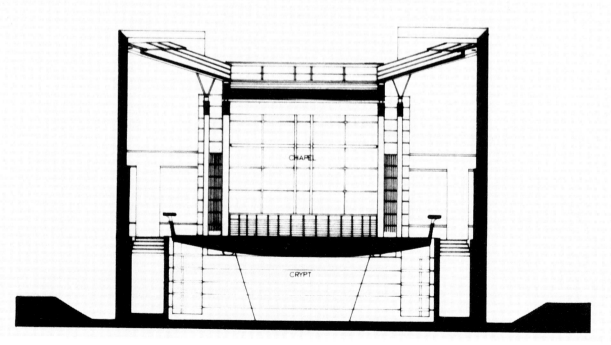

'At some stage the thing became round, but I can't quite remember how . . . the congregational space became a sort of ship' (Richard MacCormac).

Richard MacCormac feels that the successful design process has to have periods of great intensity and emphasizes the importance of speed. 'I find there are these very hot moments as it were when things happen very quickly ... I think it's rather like juggling actually, you know one couldn't juggle very slowly over a long period.'[14] MacCormac recognizes alternating phases of quite different types of cognition in his design process, with 'periods of reflection and criticism' separating the periods of more rapid and intense thought 'which throw out propositions'. According to MacCormac there are also 'periods of testing which involve quite a different frame of mind ... and that's very difficult because you very quickly see what is wrong with your proposition but you have to be very cool and careful to investigate it'. Richard MacCormac notes how 'these different frames of mind involve different instruments for producing or representing what you are doing' ranging from felt-tip pens for idea generation to a 2H pencil for testing and 'getting dimensions right'.[15]

Richard MacCormac clearly believes in both the evolutionary and revolutionary approach to the development of design ideas. However, he does believe specifically in the generation of alternatives as a conscious and deliberate discipline in the design process. Rather, he thinks he senses something in the nature of the problem which governs whether or not the generation of alternatives is a suitable strategy:

There are certain kinds of programme that structure the design very much ... and you have a sense that unless you explore options you are going to miss some tricks, whereas in other cases for example the St John's College competition, which we won, I rushed headlong as it were into an idea for the project which enthralled the client and which was quite different to the other submissions.'[16]

MacCormac has generally worked on relatively small-scale architecture. A great deal of his early work was housing, and much of the later work of the practice has been on a residential scale. He reflects that this is accidental rather than deliberate and thinks that 'what happens to people in architectural practice is fortuitous really, certain sorts of work come your way'. He does not think he set out to be a particular kind of architect, and resists attempts to classify his work in stylistic terms. 'Architecture is not about style, but, like politics, is an art of the possible, forged out of necessity and driven by the weather of commercial, economic and political aspiration' (MacCormac, 1991).[17] He enjoys making references to the past in his work and always sees them as subordinated to some greater organizing idea. 'Our sense of the past and our traditions depends very much on transforming them somehow and making them part of something new.' Richard MacCormac would probably prefer to be thought of as a craftsman rather than a philosopher. He believes in making architecture accessible but recognizes that the realization of this objective involves a deep and often agonizing struggle in what he calls 'this medium of thought':

Style is both the internal discipline of design and a means of external communication. The psychological error of the Modern Movement was to confuse these aspects by assuming that the values which sustained it would be self-evident to the external world.

[14] Speed of working

The image of the designer as a juggler is also used by Michael Wilford, and the need to oscillate very quickly between many issues is also referred to by Richard Burton. The intense concentration need to keep several moving objects in your eye at once seems to offer a parallel to the need to keep several important but quite separate issues in mind when designing. Like juggling, this requires considerable practice and preparation, and looks easy when done by an experienced practitioner so that we fail to see just how difficult a skill it is until we try it for ourselves.

[15] Analysis, synthesis and evaluation

The conventional shorthand for what Richard MacCormac is talking about here is that of 'analysis, synthesis and evaluation'. However, this is a rather more subtle and realistic description of design in action than can be found in most books of design methods. It is particularly interesting that MacCormac talks about the use of different drawing implements for each of his types of cognition. The holding of each implement in the hand and the way it makes a mark on paper can therefore be seen to condition the appropriate cognitive response. Quite simply, this helps to put the designer in the right mood for the task in hand. This is probably much more important than it may sound, since one of the great problems of managing creativity lies in developing the ability to undergo these changes at will. Much of the literature on creative thinking, lateral thinking, brainstorming, synectics and the like deals with artificial ways of engineering this change of cognitive mood. See also Robert Venturi's description of alternating between reality and fantasy.

[16] Alternatives

This represents a rather more cautious view on the generation of alternatives than that which is expressed by Eva Jiricna and Michael Wilford and, to some extent, Richard Burton. They all advocate the deliberate generation of alternatives as a conscious act followed by a selection process. Richard MacCormac is not so sure and seems to be telling us that some design problems are, in his view, amenable to this kind of approach while others are not. Unfortunately, he is not able to tell us exactly how to distinguish between them, although Denise Scott Brown suggests one possible explanation.

[17] Style

This is one of our most common responses. Few of our designers like the style-based taxonomy of architectural critics. They tell us that they do not think along stylistic lines, which might be slightly surprising to the lay public who seem to hear a great deal about 'style wars' these days. Perhaps the critics have got something to answer for here by creating a way of looking at design that, on the evidence of this book, does not seem to reflect how design is practised.

The detailed resolution of the junction between the upper floor 'vessel' and its supporting structure were the stimulus to the final understanding of the main design concept.

Richard MacCormac

Bibliography

Blundell-Jones, P. (1992). Holy vessel. *Architects' Journal*, (1 July) 24–37.

Dowson, P., and MacCormac, R. (1990). How architects design: design delegation. *Architects' Journal*, **192**(25-26), 28–41.

Goulden, G. (1977). Design for a living. *Building*, **232**(6985), 59–63.

MacCormac, R. (1978). Housing and the dilemma of style. *Architectural Review*, **163**(974), 202–206.

MacCormac, R. (1983). Arguments for modern architecture. *RIBA Transaction*, **3**, 74–84.

MacCormac, R. (1983). Urban Reform: MacCormac's manifesto. *Architects' Journal*, **177**(23), 59–77.

MacCormac, R. (1984). Actions and experience of design. *Architects' Journal*, **179** (1 and 2), 43–47.

MacCormac, R. (1985). Art of invention. *Architects' Journal*, **181**(17), 40–41.

MacCormac, R. (1987). Fitting in offices. *Architectural Review*, **185**(1083), 62–67.

MacCormac, R. (1991). The pursuit of quality. *RIBA Journal*, September, 33–41.

MacCormac, R., and Jamieson, P. (1977). MacCormac and Jamieson. *Architectural Design*, **47**(9/10), 675–706.

Pearce, D. (1986). Profile: Richard MacCormac. *The Architect*, **93**(4), 44–46.

Weston, R. (1990). Phased Faculty. *Architects' Journal*, **191**(5), 33–48.

John Outram

John Outram was born into a British military family and spent his early years in the India of the British Empire. A boyhood fascination with aircraft and flight led him to train as a pilot with the Royal Air Force, while his architectural education was gained at Regent Street Polytechnic and the AA, graduating in 1960.

His early professional experience was with the Architect's Department of the Greater London Council, Fitzroy Robinson and Lois de Soissons. He set up his own practice, John Outram Associates, in 1973 in London and has taught at the AA, the Royal College of Art and Cambridge University, as well as writing and speaking about his approach to architecture.

John Outram's architectural development can be seen to have many influences, beginning with the imperialist engineering of British India, a deep fascination with all things aeronautical, through the Modern Movement to a more recent interest in the semiology of architecture and urban form. He has argued for a rejection of the Modern Movement and the vision of buildings as machines as exemplified by 'Hi-tech' architects. He also rejects the superficiality of much 'post-modern' architecture and has argued that buildings should be both poetic and symbolic. He has also developed a highly practical approach to the construction of buildings, inventing a kind of exposed crushed brick-aggregate concrete which he calls 'Blitzcrete'.

He has called his approach to design 'popular classicism', which is a suitably contradictory phrase with which to encapsulate this unique combination of influences. His work has been attracting considerable attention and some of his completed projects such as the pumping station on the Isle of Dogs in London's Docklands have been widely published.

John Outram has become known in recent years for a highly individual approach to architecture. His work is frequently visually quite startling and instantly recognizable, with the first impact often made by the rather more decorated surfaces than we have been used to in recent times. This work is, however, backed up by a carefully, if not painstakingly, developed theory of form, space and surface which is entirely of John's devising. His practice is to be found near Regent's Park and almost a stone's throw from the Royal Institute of British Architects. Even within the office itself, the walls are decorated with drawings, posters, wall-hangings and other devices for attracting and directing the eye. These clues as to John Outram's interests are born out by an examination of both his architecture and his theoretical writing.

The practice has varied between a strength of two and 25 over the last decade, and John Outram feels that the structure and organization of it has changed slightly with its size. The practice tends to work on a small number of large projects with virtually no small-scale work. Recently they have developed a studio-based approach to the start of a project, with all staff giving their attention to the new problem. 'When a project comes in we hold an esquisse, everybody in the office does a design.' This competitive approach is used to generate a range of ideas, which provides a variety of alternatives that must still all fit within the Outram approach. This carefully calculated method reflects John Outram's belief that it is possible to generate and harness a considerable amount of energy early in the design process. 'I have always felt that you must attract as much energy as you can out of people and definitely [our recent work] is a synthesis of everyone's idea in the practice.'[1]

This great variety of ideas generated within the design office has previously been resolved into one proposal to put forward to the client. However, more recently the practice has actually presented several proposals when working on an invited competition basis:

We have actually won our first competition [using this approach] and we are negotiating another now. My three associates and I each presented a design to the client ... I thought this was quite dangerous ... but in fact it had a very good effect on the client because it winkled out of the client what he was somehow looking for, which meant that we could identify much better what the client was thinking about and therefore relate it to what we could offer.[2]

This device seems to work for John Outram perhaps because of the context within which he designs and makes his presentation. Both are based on clearly developed theories and sets of principles so that the client is faced not just with the solution but also with the process which has generated that solution. It is possible that in this context therefore the client is happy to see alternatives which nevertheless adhere to a common set of principles. This also enables Outram to be open and honest about his architectural expertise, leaving him free to admit his ignorance about the client's fundamental problem:

We said we were frankly rather confused, and that we didn't know anything about shopping centres and we were offering all these different ideas. This didn't seem to affect our client's belief in us and it enabled us to produce the first design with a much surer sense of what the client was looking for.

John Outram also believes in extending this principle of involvement beyond the boundaries of the practice itself. 'I respect ideas from wherever

[1] **Office size and structure**
The lack of small-scale work to fill the gaps probably accounts for the fluctuating size of the office here, since it will need to shrink and grow as the larger jobs come and go. As with the other single principal practices in this book, John Outram seems to keep an eye on all the jobs currently in the office. The idea of taking all staff away from their current duties to work on a new project as an esquisse is probably less dramatic than it sounds, given the way in which this particular practice works.

[2] **Alternatives**
This presentation of alternative designs to the client is a controversial theme for our designers. It seems to be based on the notion that a conversation with the client mediated by the presence of proposed solutions can elicit more information than a purely abstract discussion about the problem, as suggested by the traditional view of the briefing process. Michael Wilford shares a similar view, though Ken Yeang strongly cautions against this. However, John Outram's is the only practice actually to operate on this basis of alternatives generated not by an appointed design team but rather by the whole office.

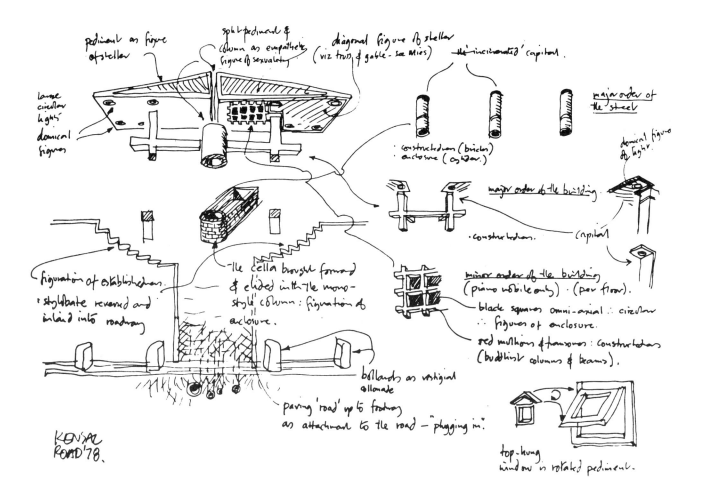

KENSAL
ROAD '78.

John Outram's early design process was based on the concepts of 'shelteredness', 'enclosedness', 'constructedness', and 'establishedness'. Here these concepts were applied to his small business units in Kensal Road, London. The result was effectively a new architectual order which he called the Kensal Order.

they come, obviously they come from structural engineers, mechanical engineers, the clients themselves ... '[3] This represents a clear view of design as a controlled social act. '[Our process] proves that architecture is a collaborative process, which isn't to say that I am not ultimately in control because I am.'[4]

He is able to retain this overall or ultimate control through a very detailed and explicitly stated process to which the whole practice adheres. 'I've evolved a design vocabulary like a design language, which can cope with all this diverse input because in the end it all gets translated into the Outram architecture.' Of course, in order for this process to work, all his design staff must learn to 'speak' this Outram language. 'The longer they stay, the more adept they get, if they refuse to speak it at all then there is a mutual parting, as it were.' While speaking with great personal passion about his design language John Outram has developed a remarkably mature and sophisticated view of the way his staff relate to this constraint:

The staff who get on best are the ones who regard it like another aspect of the game that they are required to play, you know. There is the district surveyor, there's the quantity surveyor, there's the structural engineer and there's John Outram.[5]

John Outram has been developing his process for some time and claims now to be 'getting a long way towards understanding it'. His interest has tended to move from elevations through space and form towards surface decoration. 'It's a sort of cumulative process ... now I am particularly interested in ornament which is because I've sort of achieved an understanding of form if you like.' He claims originally to have 'worked out a rather basic design process' over 30 years ago but feels that only really dealt with buildings, whereas his current process is rather more sophisticated and can also cope with the urban context.

The current process as used and described by John Outram involves a series of stages. The exact meaning and application of these stages to the problem is by no means transparent, partly due to the rather unconventional nature of Outram's ideas:

We have this rather elaborate process in seven stages ... they provide the theory behind the design ... I need to go through these stages and consider them and decide how much of them we will develop ... when I critique people's inputs I can talk to them about it in these terms.

These 'seven stages' are in fact a series of issues which Outram considers it essential to include in a scheme. Although there is an implied sequence or progression in the list, this is not necessarily rigidly adhered to. In fact John Outram refers to these stages as 'rites' in order to express them as performances or acts and to distinguish them from the mythology which surrounds them in his thoughts. Many of John Outram's seven stages make resonances with what others have written before about the process of creating architecture. They tend to be connected by an overarching concern with the relationship between architecture and the natural, perhaps even primeval, landscape. What is special here is that, together, these seven rites form not only a theory of architecture but, more importantly, a process which is actually in use by an active practice. In fact Outram claims that the theory grew out of the practice rather than the other way round:

[3]The central idea and the design team
It is worth noting here that on the Judge Institute building, the structural engineer said of working with John Outram, 'He involves the whole design team in the concept', and the services engineer confirmed this by saying 'He's very receptive to ideas and involves you from an early stage rather than just expecting you to fit in afterwards'. (See Stungo, 1993.)

[4]The design team
One of the most popular themes in this book is the extent to which our designers emphasize this point. Critics and the media tend to personalize and develop the cult of the individual, perhaps for their own purposes. This, together with the 'style wars' view of design, seem to be the two big myths of our time, both generated by the media and both consistently denied by the designers studied here.

[5]Guiding principles
John Outram's guiding principles are so well developed that they have been expanded into what he describes as a design process. They are also so well documented that they have even formed the basis of an exhibition at the Venice Biennale. One of the variations to be found among the design practices in this book is the extent to which they operate a practice theme. John Outram's practice could be seen to have the strongest of all, with an elaborate theory and process laid down. Eva Jiricna seems to control this in a similar way. Others like Ken Yeang have a strong process and overall theme but allow much greater variety of action and thought among the individual designers themselves. John Outram's 'ultimate control' is probably only made possible by the extent to which he has articulated his theory and process.

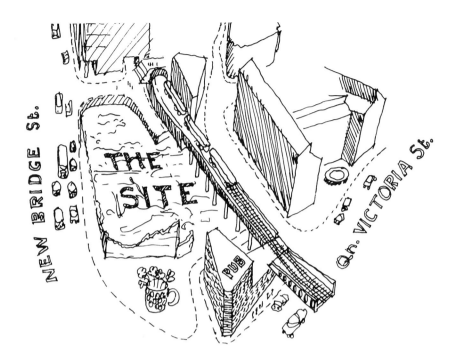

This and page 77 show the next stage in the development of John Outram's design process at a site in Blackfriars London. This design process was based on what John Outram has described as seven rites. They are: 'grove' 'cenotaph', 'cataclysm', 'entablement'. 'valley', 'inscription' and 'facade'.

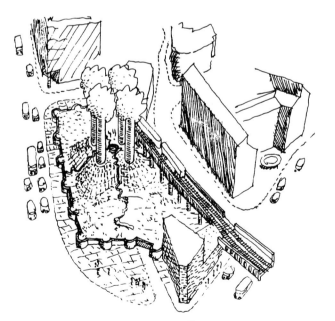

First Rite : Grove.

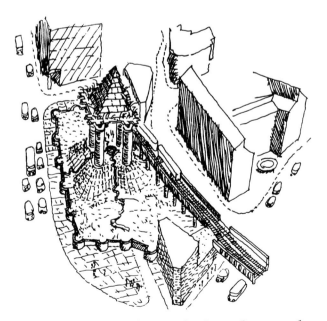

Second Rite : Cenotaph.

I am proposing these ideas, but the theory is now getting ahead of the practice whereas previously the practice was ahead of the theory ... There was a sort of fictional phase in which I looked back at my first two buildings and reproduced them in words and then took out of those a structure of visual metaphors because for two years I just couldn't do the drawings I wanted to communicate what was in those buildings.[6]

In Outram's earlier process he gave his buildings the characteristics he wanted by concentrating on what he called 'sheltered-ness', 'constructed-ness', 'enclosed-ness', and 'established-ness'.[7] These very basic and fundamental qualities enabled him to design facades and even buildings, whereas he feels the recent and more sophisticated version enables him to work on buildings and cities.

These seven stages or rites in John Outram's current process are: 'the grove', 'the cenotaph', ' cataclysm', 'the entablement', 'the valley', 'the inscription', and 'the facade'. A more detailed description of the meaning of these rites is to be found in John Outram's own writing and was perhaps most explored most thoroughly in his submission for the Venice Biennale in 1991. We shall therefore have to be content with a rather brief summary here using John Outram's own words: 'The recovery of the 'grove' is what Corb does when he lifts up the buildings and finds the jungle underneath. [Although Outram parts company with Le Corbusier by trying to 'retain rather than destroy the urban terrain.'] The translation of the 'grove' into the 'cenotaph' or a sort of tomb ... and then there is the burial of the cenotaph in the city itself, which is what you actually build ['cataclysm'] ... Then follows the recapitulation of the 'grove' through the reconstruction of the table [Outram refers to this as the 'entablement' formed by the city inundating the grove-temple up to its roof] ... Next there is the folding of a valley which connects the landscape of the 'entablement' with the floor of the city ... Then there is the rite of 'inscription' which is writing over the surfaces ... and the last stage is that of the 'facade' which is representing what has been going on inside on the outside of the building.'

These ideas are fundamental indeed. Outram is tugging at some chords in the depths of our conscious appreciation of architecture here, and in order not to constrain his design process his discussion of these ideas remains fairly abstract. In fact they can most easily be understood by studying his buildings, which is perhaps just as he would like it. However, Outram is also quite realistic about the nature of people's response to his architecture. He does not expect that users of his building will understand all his theories, nor does he feel this is necessary to achieve his objectives. 'I am arguing the reverse, that it is sufficient for most people that they know there is a meaning, this enables them to engage with the architect at whatever level they choose.' When talking or writing about his work John Outram makes few intellectual concessions to his audience and in consequence his text requires careful study. However, he strongly disapproves of exclusive and over-precious attitudes towards art in general but particularly towards architecture:

There is an elitist attitude to art which says that if anybody appreciates it without understanding it can't be any good. You just can't expect to build cities with that kind of programme; it's unrealistic and very foolish. Public art has got to be appreciated by people who are not literary, who don't know anything about it ... this is recognized in a way by the Marxist modernism in which we were

[6] Conceptualizing
John Outram's process displays an extreme form of this need to develop ideas more in terms of a philosophical literary medium before visualization. Ian Ritchie follows a similar path which leads in quite a different direction visually. See also Eva Jiricna's description of exchanging ideas with the client verbally before using images, and Richard MacCormac's use of verbal conceptualizing.

[7] Symbolism
The development of John Outram's theory and process helps us to understand his overall philosophy here. What is common to all John's work and to both versions of his theory and process is an overall concern with the meanings we attach to the built environment. These early ideas concentrated on the way a building 'explained' its existence, purpose and construction to its users. As can be seen from the next paragraph, John Outram has now extended this to cover the building sitting in its urban landscape, but the basic concerns remain the same.

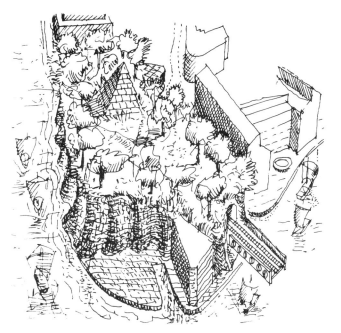

Third Rite : Cataclysm

Fourth Rite : Entablement.

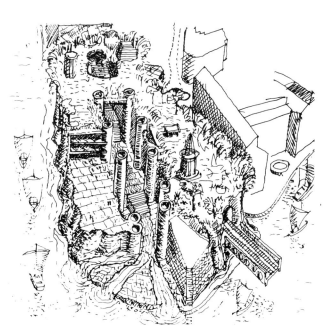

Fifth Rite : Valley.

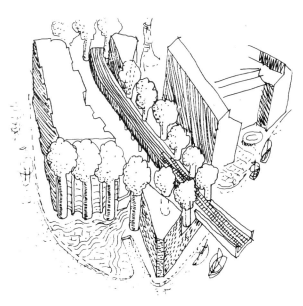

Seventh Rite : Facade.

taught that there must not be any literary content, but I think that is a mistake – the literary content must be there but it must not be necessary to its enjoyment.[8]

So John Outram's design process can be seen to provide him with a rather sophisticated kind of checklist which raises for him all the key issues about the levels of meaning architecture should have. This is not because he insists that his clients or users should necessarily understand the mythology behind his creation. Rather, he fervently believes that such a process gives rise to an architecture which is generally understandable and that people want architecture to respect some constant characteristics which have become part of our collective consciousness. 'You can't deny the sort of residue that people have, the residual feeling that a building is one lump on another.' However, the clever trick engineered by John Outram's process is to avoid the sterility of mere reproduction. 'I've drawn up a technique which retained its [the city's] comfortableness but which displaced it in the imagination with imaginative strategies.'[9]

John Outram likes his work to have layers of meaning, perhaps with varying levels of accessibility. This obsession is taken down by his process below the level of form and space to that of surface and material. He is deeply interested in pure design and is currently particularly concerned with the 'inscription' part of his process, which leads him to investigate materials that reveal their construction on the surface. In fact John Outram is also a very sound technologist. He has developed a material which he calls 'Blitzcrete', which consists of a kind of concrete made with crushed brick aggregate which then has its surface ground down by 2 to 3 mm. He argues that 'a beautiful material is like a pebbly beach. It has many layers of texture and colour.' In fact Outram has developed a palette of materials based on fairly cheap precast moulded concrete technology but which have inlaid and self-coloured surfaces that are rich in texture and capable of weathering gracefully.

Technology is to be found in abundance in John Outram's office, with computers sitting alongside more traditional drawing equipment. His attitude towards this is nicely illustrated by his explanation of how important colour is to him during the design process. 'I have two boxes, one is full of coloured pens and the other is full of coloured crayons which together with the colour copier make a sort of design technology.' This technology allows him to use colour even in working drawings, making use of both symbolic and representational and compositional colour. In fact he thinks of architecture 'as solid colour', and found this one of the aspects of his work 'most difficult to model', before the acquisition of the colour copier.[10]

John Outram never allows his undoubted natural technical ability to dominate his design process. His formative experiences as a child and later in early adult life as an aircraft pilot leave him perfectly comfortable with advanced technology, but he believes that it is inappropriate to apply this to architecture. 'An aeroplane has to have this quality of dynamic flexibility, it has to work upside down and so on, but a building doesn't and it seems irrational and unnatural to design buildings in this way.' Instead, John Outram views structural elements at several levels, as with all aspects of his architecture. For example, he describes some pieces of blue concrete with integral white spirals as 'logs'. 'They are certainly beams, they are kind of rafts as well which takes them off into another level of iconography where they are like flying carpets or rafts floating about in the sea.' Outram's buildings then are generally very solid and often massive. But he likes to play with often unclear thoughts about the

[8]**Interpretation**
There are possibly two strands to Outram's argument here. First, that art is imbued with certain qualities as a result of being driven by a coherent theory of ideas, even if those ideas themselves are not communicated. Second, that art, more specifically architecture, can communicate directly with deep feelings and ideas which may themselves not be explicitly appreciated by the perceiver. Public and client reaction to John Outram's buildings would seem so far to support these notions.

[9]**Technology**
John Outram is himself an interesting mixture in being entirely at home in the world of engineering and yet feeling strongly that this should not be allowed to become a primary generator of architecture. He shares this view with Robert Venturi and Michael Wilford.

[10]**Computer-aided design and drawing**
This eclectic attitude towards the technology of the design office seems to be one John Outram shares with Ian Ritchie and Robert Venturi. Perhaps it is only when one feels a master of advanced technology that one can feel free to mix it with low technology. The doubts that many designers express about computers seems to suggest that they fear such technology must take over the entire process. Clearly this is not necessarily so.

An important part of John Outram's architectural design process is the incorporation of technology as an integral part of the design of the 'order'. Here and on page 81 his sketches of three orders for the same scheme show different ways of housing services resulting in different but related architectural expression.

relationship between mass and weight. 'Mass without weight' is one of his favourite phrases:

I often design buildings which look as if they are weighty with columns and beams and so on, and yet I like to deny that, I like to say weight is just another metaphor ... We know that buildings are heavy and solid but ... I want the wall to mean something, I want to write on it, I want it to be patterned, I want it to be hollow and to contain services.

Just as he refuses to allow technology to dominate his process, so John Outram denies the functional principles of the Modern Movement:

There is nothing absolute about deriving architecture from functional manipulation. When you look at a plan by Corb, these wonderful shapes that he has rationalized out of bathroom and things, I mean they are magic really, they are completely magical diagrams but I would much rather have the magic without the spurious functionality in the way.[11]

Paradoxically, Outram shares much territory with Le Corbusier, in particular his belief in the value of relating form to the natural world and of the ordering effects of classical proportioning systems and, above all, the value of a theory of design. What, however, Outram seems to have achieved is a connection between his theory and his process which gives rise to a form of architecture that is instantly recognizable and seems to appeal to ordinary people while retaining its uncompromising intellectual programme.

[11]**Radical constraints**
There is absolutely no doubt about John Outram's view of the Modern Movement tradition of designing buildings by planning their basic functions and organizing form and space from these considerations. Perhaps Outram represents the most extreme position on this to be found in this book. He certainly would not agree that 'the plan is the generator'.

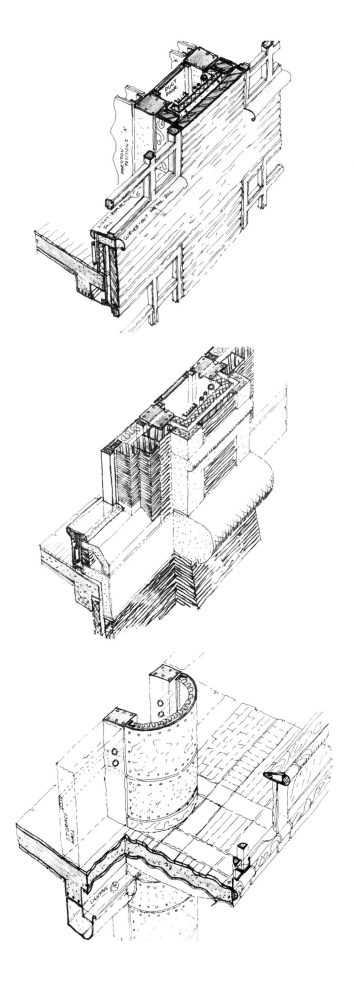

John Outram

Bibliography

Buchanan, P. (1981). Street-wise: Metaphors of the city. *Architectural Review*, **169**(1008), 76–85.

Buchanan, P. (1986). House and harp. *Architectural Review*, **179**(1072), 62–69.

Glancey, J. (1983). Flight from Utopia. *Blueprint*, **19** July/August, 24–26.

Glancey, J. (1986). Brickworks. *Architects' Journal*, **184**(44), 12–15.

Guest, P. (1991). BeWhiching Outram. *Building*, 10 May, 18–22.

Outram, J. (1983). Supermarket forces. *Architectural Review*, **173**(1035), 69–73.

Outram, J. (1984). Uses and abuses of Arcadia. *Architectural Review*, **175**(1084), 76–80.

Outram, J. (1985). Urban workshops. *Building Supplement*, **249**(7404), 31–35.

Outram, J. (1988). Opium of the masses. *AJ Focus*, **1**(11), 46–47.

Outram, J. (1988). St. Pauls: an architect's reflection. *Landscape*, 5 February, 42–45.

Outram, J. (1990). Mass without weight. *Concrete Quarterly*, Autumn, 2–4.

Pearce, D., and Outram, J. (1986). Profile: John Outram. *RIBA Journal*, **83**(1), 5–8.

Powell, K. (1988). Popular classicism. *Country Life*, **182**(33), 62–65.

Stungo, N. (1993). Cambridge first. *Building*, **CCLVIII**(14), 18–21.

Turnbull, D. (1988). Temple of storms. *Architects' Journal*, **188**(42), 58–63.

Ian Ritchie

Ian Ritchie was born in Hove on the south coast of England. He studied architecture at the Polytechnic of Central London where he graduated with distinction in 1972. He worked for Foster Associates on such seminal buildings as the Willis Faber and Dumas Office and the Sainsbury Centre for the Visual Arts. Fosters was then quite a small office and Ian Ritchie has always preferred small organizations. He left in 1976 to build his much-acclaimed house at Fluy near Amiens in France, a country with which he has many links. He has collaborated with a number of other influential figures, including research and development work on a short-span aluminium structural prototype for Michael Hopkins. In particular, in 1972 he started working with Martin Francis, an industrial designer and naval architect. From 1978 he also collaborated with the engineer Peter Rice, who asked him to act as a design consultant to the lightweight structures group at Ove Arup and Partners.

In 1979 Ian Ritchie joined with Michael Davies and Alan Stanton, who had worked with Richard Rogers on the Pompidou Centre, to form Chrysalis Architects London. In 1981 Peter Rice, Martin Francis and Ian Ritchie formed RFR in Paris and they began work on the National Museum of Science, Technology and Industry at La Villette.

Ian Ritchie Architects, as it is now structured, was also formed in 1981 in London although a considerable amount of its work has been completed across the Channel in France. Ian Ritchie has worked on a number of French cultural buildings, individual houses as well as housing, underground railway stations for London Transport, office buildings including one at Stockley Park and various other building types. His work has been widely published both in books and journals and has been exhibited mainly in England and France.

Ian Ritchie has lectured widely on his own work and attitudes to design, and is currently writing a book. He has taught at a number of institutes, including the Polytechnic of Central London, the Architectural Association and the University of Sheffield.

Ian Ritchie's attitude towards the size and organization of his design office sounds very simple. He claims this is 'about the numbers of people who can basically communicate well together'. The number five figures strongly in his calculations, which are actually quite sophisticated in their resolution. He feels groups of up to five work well on a design and he runs five such groups directed by associates handling the larger projects, while smaller jobs are directed by experienced staff.[1] Ian himself feels able to keep close track of about five jobs. The result is a staff of 20 to 25 people who, Ian says 'can actually all discuss around a table, especially when someone has a birthday'. He was worried when the office got larger a few years ago that he 'sensed a breaking down of the quality, social relationships, and everything else'. So important is this idea to Ian Ritchie that he has kept to groups of five even when under pressure from clients to put more staff onto a job to meet deadlines. Ian rarely runs a job himself. 'The commitment we make to quality requires a very much day-in day-out relationship with clients and consultants and everybody else, and I can't do that if I am running a job.'[2]

The emphasis here is very much on quality control exercised very personally by him, but mediated through an extremely relaxed and informal atmosphere which, like many things here, is more sophisticated than may appear at first sight. There are no separate offices in the converted top floor of a Docklands wharf building. This, together with the careful calculations on the size of the social group, seems to break down the apparently hierarchical structure into one in which it is clear where authority lies and yet where all feel able to contribute and generate ideas. Ian Ritchie thinks it has a 'Californian feel' and frequently mentions the pleasure he gets from designing. Talking to him, it is obvious that maintaining the pleasure and the quality of his work is his major driving and motivating force.

For Ian Ritchie the design process begins with an attempt to construct a working relationship with his client. Before even discussing architecture, he tries to lead the client into his process:

It is very rare for a client to commission a building more than once in his life, except in the commercial sector. There is nobody who ever trains a single client on how to commission or deal with an architect. The first move is to talk through the brief, understand what has led to it, understand fundamentally what it is about.

That conversation about the brief, which he always questions, is primarily used by Ian Ritchie to build up the client's level of confidence and trust in him.[3] 'It is not about buildings, it's not about solutions or ideas about buildings.'

From this stage Ian Ritchie moves to what he calls 'pre-conceptual thinking', which also precedes any ideas about buildings. These concepts are more poetic and may have many different origins. Some are to do with the site, some with the client and others actually with the purpose of the building. In the case of his house at Eagle Rock this idea emerged from the site, from the shape of a rock and from the idea of flight. In fact here both client and architect really found the site so beautiful that ideally they would have preferred never to create any architecture at all! When thinking about a French cultural centre Ian Ritchie talks about the mayor of the town, and of the political statement he was making by commissioning the building. When approaching the design of smoke vents for a London Underground station the pre-conceptual idea was about the movement of air. 'We came down to air and it wasn't the pragmatic and practical

[1]**The design team**
This size of about five seems to offer a comfortable size of group for designing. Perhaps this is because it nicely balances the opposing requirements of keeping communications simple and direct and yet having a wide range of ideas available in the group.

[2]**Office size and structure**
This size of about two dozen staff seems quite common in practices led by a single principal. Herman Hertzberger, Eva Jiricna and John Outram all expressed a wish to have the practice about this size. They also follow a similar pattern to Ian Ritchie in not running any one job themselves but being involved in all. This can be compared with the larger practices in this book that are partnerships in which the partners all lead for particular jobs or take corporate roles.

[3]**The client**
See also the comments by Herman Hertzberger, Eva Jiricna and Robert Venturi about the importance of establishing trust between designer and client.

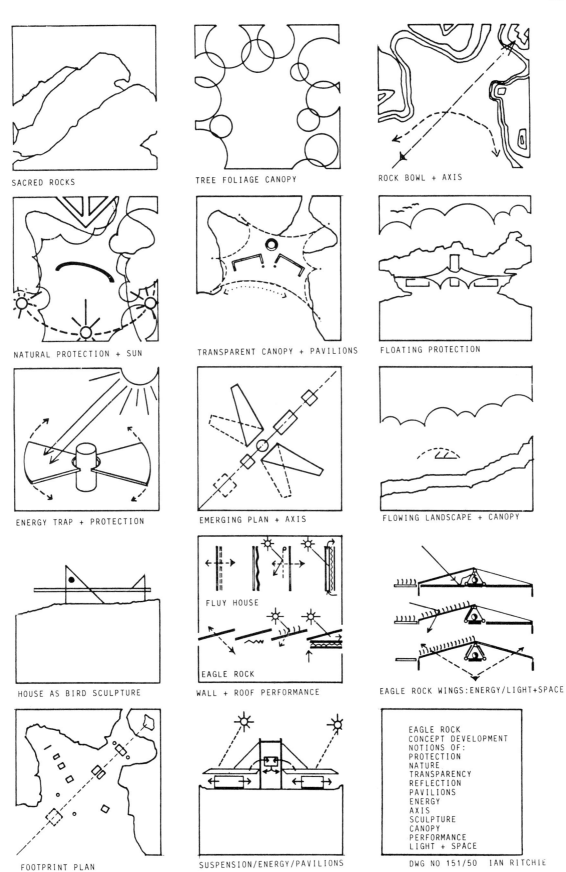

SACRED ROCKS

TREE FOLIAGE CANOPY

ROCK BOWL + AXIS

NATURAL PROTECTION + SUN

TRANSPARENT CANOPY + PAVILIONS

FLOATING PROTECTION

ENERGY TRAP + PROTECTION

EMERGING PLAN + AXIS

FLOWING LANDSCAPE + CANOPY

HOUSE AS BIRD SCULPTURE

FLUY HOUSE

EAGLE ROCK

WALL + ROOF PERFORMANCE

EAGLE ROCK WINGS:ENERGY/LIGHT+SPACE

FOOTPRINT PLAN

SUSPENSION/ENERGY/PAVILIONS

EAGLE ROCK
CONCEPT DEVELOPMENT
NOTIONS OF:
PROTECTION
NATURE
TRANSPARENCY
REFLECTION
PAVILIONS
ENERGY
AXIS
SCULPTURE
CANOPY
PERFORMANCE
LIGHT + SPACE

DWG NO 151/50   IAN RITCHIE

An example of Ian Ritchie's 'pre-conceptual thinking' as applied to his design for a house at Eagle Rock.

issues about how to move air, but would air provide us with the central notion of how we could develop a concept for a building?' Ian Ritchie thinks this early, poetic thinking should be taught more in schools of architecture as a way of 'conceiving and being subversive'.

Pre-conceptual ideas are discussed by yet another of Ian Ritchie's groups of five, but this time the composition of the group is variable. Sometimes it might be the five design team leaders, and sometimes a group spanning the depth of his loose hierarchy. Again there is a very personal control operating here, with Ian Ritchie himself retiring to his 'kitchen table in the early hours of the morning' where he does his private thinking and doodling.[4]

Ian Ritchie seems to invest a substantial amount of time and mental effort into understanding these early notions, and often seems to reach this understanding through concise verbal concepts. He talks about how when designing his glass houses at La Villette in Paris he only gradually came to realize that the notion of 'transparency' was at the heart of his obsession:

It wasn't about material. It was about how do you define transparency? It took us quite a long time, and in the end we decided that we had to play something on a clear surface to tell you it was there. The irony is that when you use glass and you're perpendicular to it, it's magic, but as soon as you're oblique it's opaque.

They worked away at the practical issues of structure and maintenance and, of course, cost, and Ian Ritchie worried they were losing the pre-conceptual idea somehow with a large square-braced grid to hold up the glass wall. Eventually he realized that the notion of 'panorama' was missing and that this implied horizontality:

It suddenly twigged on me that part of the transparency was panorama. If you had transparency and you had panorama then you've got it![5]

Eventually these pre-conceptual ideas turn into ideas about actual buildings, but Ian Ritchie sees this process as a continuing battle:

It is very easy to imagine that if you have this generator it will automatically come out at the other end as a building, but it's not true. You have to keep working very hard at it.

This pre-conceptual idea turning into what has been called a 'primary generator' serves another almost even more important purpose for Ian Ritchie:

Unless there is enough power and energy in this generative concept, you will actually not produce a very good end result, because there is this three years or so of hard work to go through and the only sustenance apart from the bonhomie of the people involved is the quality of this idea, that is the food. It's the thing that nourishes, that keeps you, you know every time you get bored or fed up or whatever you can go back and get an injection from it, and the strength of that idea is fundamental, it has to carry an enormous amount of energy.[6]

A review of Ian Ritchie's architecture gives the impression of a fairly 'high-tech' approach. Certainly there is very little use of brick and tile in his work and even as early as his acclaimed house at Eagle Rock there appears to be a 'look, no hands' view of structure. His more recent use of

[4]Drawing
Herman Hertzberger describes a similar process of retiring away from the office in the evening and sketching on his beloved A3 pad. This seems to reflect a need to alternate between the hurly-burly of the office where ideas are rapidly exchanged and the quiet of the home at night where personal thoughts can be examined in a more reflective mood.

[5]Conceptualizing
Ian Ritchie talks with great animation about these ideas and it seems that the need to resolve them in his own mind is extremely strong and provides a powerful motivating force in his work.

[6]Sense of purpose
What Ian Ritchie is reminding us of here is that the reality of design, certainly in architecture, is that it is a long and painful process to bring an idea to fruition. Watching research students working for three years on a doctorate reminds us that success is often dependent on some burning inner wish to resolve an issue. It seems necessary for designers to believe in the importance of resolving problems which may become extremely important to them even though they may never be made apparent to the users of their work. This refusal to accept anything less than an elegant and meaningful resolution can make such designers seem stubborn and difficult to work with. In the author's experience it is a common characteristic of good design students, who can, for this reason, occasionally go quite off the rails. Richard MacCormac makes a similar point.

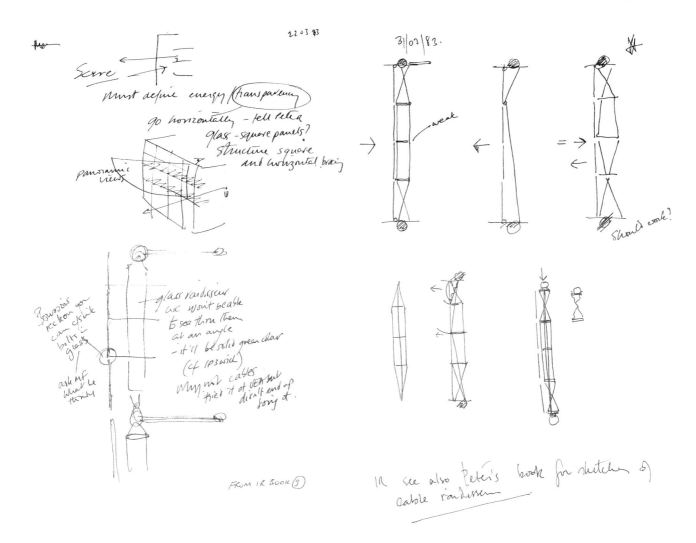

Two pages from Ian Ritchie's sketchbook exploring the ideas of transparency and panorama in the design of the glass pavillions at La Villette. The photograph shows the end result.

structural forms and extensive cooperation with the engineer Peter Rice would tend to confirm this analysis. However, Ian Ritchie is quick to disagree, and objects strongly to being labelled as a 'high-tech' stylist, nor does he feel that technology is a design generator for him. He has clearly been asked about this before and has a well-rehearsed but delightful way of describing his relationship with technology:

When people ask me this question I use an analogy. I describe this beautiful parrot sitting on my shoulder – multicoloured, very beautiful – called 'technology'. Very often he leaps off the shoulder onto the paper and shits all over it before we've actually started thinking and you have to get hold of him and stick him back up there. He is tame, he does behave himself and he doesn't always end up in the project at all, but he's there and we talk to him all the time.[7]

Ian Ritchie distinguishes between the use of technology either for its own sake or for the sake of creating an image, and his relationship with his 'parrot'. He describes this as 'real applied science' in order to achieve other more important design objectives. For example, he refused to allow the *Architectural Review* to include Eagle Rock in an issue on high-tech architecture because, in his view, it actually uses very low technology. 'It happens to have a bit of steel hanging about, but it's plasterboard inside, it's plywood, it's nails, half of it was put up by students who were working here!'

Even so, Ian Ritchie is clearly very interested in modern materials. He is fascinated by, if not obsessed with, glass, about which he talks in an almost unbelieving way. 'If I had invented it I would describe it as a material you can't see, but it keeps the rain out and it keeps the heat in and you would think "what is it, what is it?" but it's actually there and it's a question of finding it I suppose.' This search for 'what glass is' seems to pervade much of Ian's work, but even here he would claim this is more of a poetic search than one of pure technology. He describes how at the Paris Air Show he became fascinated by titanium castings used for aircraft components, and how he compared this with the traditional fittings in greenhouses. The research that followed was, however, again not technology for its own sake but an attempt to realize his more poetic notions about transparency. Ian Ritchie returns to his image of the parrot called 'technology' to explain this:

There's a little one on the other shoulder called 'art' or 'poetry', he's very powerful, squeaks a lot but he's not got the nerve of this one yet and that's because we are still maturing into that field. It's only a few years since we've been working hard at it so it doesn't feel comfortable yet.[8]

This presents a rather sophisticated and complex view of a designer developing and maturing. It is a picture which is seldom portrayed in the current battle of styles, which does not interest Ritchie. He strives for quality, not a style. Ian Ritchie has himself clearly grown out of the Modern Movement, with its attention to the functional and its emphasis on the expression of the technology. In describing his approach Ian Ritchie often refers to poetry. This ties in with his use of the notion of pre-conceptual ideas, for the origins of his work are not architectural and not even visual but more philosophical. An example of this thinking is in the way he describes his friend and collaborator Peter Rice's work in resolving Utzon's Sydney Opera House into parts of spheres. For Ritchie the original idea was 'a poetry of shape, which was not a geometrical idea, but

[7]**Technology**
This delightful image seems exactly to capture Ian Ritchie's attitude towards technology. He remains simultaneously fascinated and wary of it. The fascination, which seems a characteristic of many good designers, represents a sort of curiosity about how things might be done rather than how they have been done. The wariness comes from wanting to contain the technology to serve his higher purpose rather than dominate. Ian Ritchie's view might be contrasted with that of Michael Wilford, who feels technology to be a secondary, if not a tertiary, consideration. On the other hand, Eva Jiricna seems to use the technology of materials and joints as her primary generator.

[8]**Parallel lines of thought**
Perhaps this reflects Ian Ritchie's own origins. His education during a more stable period of 'Modern Movement' design followed by early practice in a more functionalist atmosphere mean that he has only more recently come to develop this side of his approach. However, what he also seems to be suggesting is that these two parrots represent quite different, perhaps irreconcilable, ways of looking at his design. There is no suggestion that one follows the other but rather that both parrots are free to make interventions throughout the process.

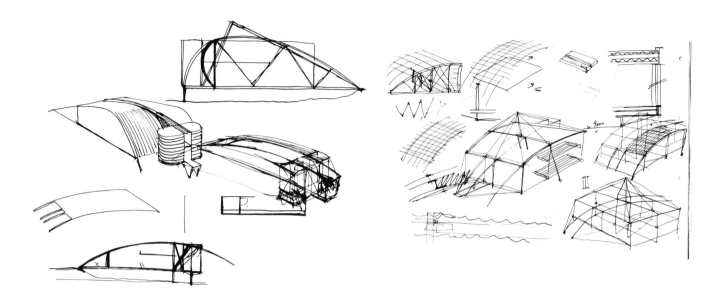

Early ideas and development of the main forms for Ian Ritchie's design for a pharmacy at Boves in France.

instead a geometry based on something else altogether, a kind of gesture of line'. Although Ritchie has used symbolic elements such as, on one occasion, arabesque geometry, this is not normally a driving force for him. It is the technology and the function of the building which for Ian Ritchie bring order to the art or poetry.

As he moves around his office Ian Ritchie carries a sketchbook which he opens and draws in as he talks. Sketches and doodles abound, together with computers and physical models, but there is little sign of the proudly presented perspectives of past work which can so often grace the walls in such design offices. Ian Ritchie explains this by admitting that they are 'very reluctant seducers by means of drawings' and agrees that designers tend to solve problems they see at least partly as a result of the way they look at their designs.[9] 'It is one of the reasons that we don't make decisions solely on drawings; models are always made and displayed and now the computer operates in that field as well.' He values each, the traditional drawing, the computer model and the physical model, for what they bring to the design process. For Ian Ritchie the computer 'can actually get you to an eye view that a model can't ... and the model offers what the computer and the freehand drawing cannot which is to let you look at the whole thing very quickly in many directions but it doesn't take you in as a human being'.

Ian Ritchie uses his computers 'very much as a sketch tool'. He believes in getting simple and quick views of emerging designs to aid design decision making. The architects look at these rather crude drawings, he feels, to solve particular problems. 'What we are looking for might be only 10% of all the lines on the screen. A particular proportion, a particular view.' Consequently he never lets clients see these drawings since they would 'see 100% of the lines' and thus miss the point.[10]

Ian Ritchie draws another simple working diagram of a triangle connecting the designers, industry and the client, in a set of relationships he works hard to sustain. 'If any one of these wobbles, we try and mend it.' But ultimately if the relationship cannot be mended Ian Ritchie prefers not to continue with the job. 'It's better to tell the client that the relationship is not working.'[11]

The more you talk to Ian Ritchie, the more of a polymath he seems to become. There can be no doubt from even a cursory glance at his architecture that he is an artist, although perhaps he would prefer to be called a poet. Advanced technology runs through most of his projects and he clearly has a fascination with the 'parrot sitting on his shoulder'. Ian Ritchie refers to his 'H cubed' model of what he looks for in his staff. He talks of using 'one's Heart, one's Head and one's Hands', which perhaps sums up his attitude towards the architectural design process as neatly as any of his phrases. It seems important to keep these all in balance.[12]

In the end perhaps Ian's greatest skill is in bringing ideas to realizable architecture through his understanding of social relationships. Immense care has been taken to set up the office structure and to create and maintain a creative relationship with clients and consultants. Thus although it remains a highly personal practice, its achievements are very much a result of Ian's own ability to get the best out of others.

[9] Drawing
This distrust of drawings as dangerously seductive is shared with Herman Hertzberger and seems an extremely mature attitude. Perhaps only good artists are able to recognize the power of drawings to mislead or even deceive!

[10] Computer-aided design
Ian Ritchie's attitude towards the technology of computers seems to parallel his view of the technology of architecture itself. He is fascinated by it but never allows this enthusiasm to become dominant. Some designers tend to use computer-aided design to impress the client, while Ian Ritchie tries to avoid showing the client these drawings. Thus we can see Ian distrustful of drawings, CAD and models. All have a role to play and perhaps only the skilled designer can judge how to use each of them. A similarly eclectic view is to be found in the chapters on John Outram and on Denise Scott Brown and Robert Venturi.

[11] The client
See the earlier note on the client and similar comments by Herman Hertzberger about abandoning a commission if the relationship with the client is wrong.

[12] Balance
It is no coincidence that many of our designers speak of this need to maintain a balance particularly between what might be called art and technology. In the language of *How Designers Think* this is a distinction between the practical and radical constraints of making things work and do a useful job, and the more formal and symbolic constraints of making them beautiful and meaningful. See, particularly, Richard Burton's comments about this for a similar attitude to Ian Ritchie.

A computer generated perspective and photograph of the finished object. Part of Ian Ritchie's Ecology Gallery for the Natural History Museum in London.

Ian Ritchie

Bibliography

Carolin, P. (1986). Near East Tower. *Architects' Journal*, **183**(12), 28–31.

Cook, P. (1983). The eagle has landed. *Architects' Journal*, **178**(43), 62–75.

Cruikshank, D. (1989). Housing with history. *Architects' Journal*, **172**(29), 24–29.

Ellis, C. (1986). Tomorrow's world. *Architects' Journal*, **183**(18), 28–37.

Finch, P. (1987). Riverside approach. *Building Design*, 13 March, 10.

Herron, R. (1990). Matter of fax: Ian Ritchie's pharmacy at Boves. *Architecture Today*, **12**, 28–33.

Lecuyer, A. (1987). Modern moves on the docks. *Architects' Journal*, **185**(15), 22–27.

Melhuish, C. (1989). Garden Centre. *Building Design*, 1 December, 15.

Pawley, M. (1991). Zero gravity. *Blueprint*, March, 28–31.

Ritchie, I. (1991). Natural selection: how CAD helped Ian Ritchie Architects design the new ecology gallery at the Natural History Museum. *Architecture Today*, **14**, 51–52.

Stevens, T. (1980). Unfolding chrysalis. *Building Design*, 12 September, 36–39.

Wright, L. (1979). Self-build at Fluy. *Architectural Review*, **166**(989), 46–49.

Robert Venturi and Denise Scott Brown

Robert Venturi was born in Philadelphia in 1925 where he now practises. He studied at Princeton University, completing a Master's thesis in 1950 on 'Context in Architectural Composition'. He was awarded a Fellowship to study at the American Academy in Rome from 1954 to 1956, where he was also to return as Architect-in-Residence in 1966. His early architectural career included periods with Louis Kahn and Eero Saarinen. He formed a partnership with John Rauch in 1964, who had qualified from the University of Pennsylvania. He has taught at the Universities of Pennsylvania and Yale.

Denise Scott Brown was born in Zambia. She studied at the Architectural Association in London followed by two Masters degrees, in planning and architecture, at the University of Pennsylvania, completing the latter in 1965. She has written and lectured extensively, including teaching at the Universities of Pennsylvania, California at Berkeley, UCLA, Yale and Harvard.

Denise Scott Brown and Robert Venturi met in 1960 and have collaborated ever since, marrying in 1967. Their practice has produced an extensive portfolio of projects, attracting many major design awards. The scale of work ranges through the decorative arts, furniture, architecture, urban design right up to planning. Their architecture, which has been widely published, ranges from the single house up to the scale of urban design, and has been designed for the United States, Europe and the Middle East and Far East.

However, they are at least as well known for their writing as for their design. Robert Venturi's book 'Complexity and Contradiction in Architecture', although published as recently as 1966, has arguably already become a classic. It is certainly one of the most significant contributions to the debate about the Post-modern Movement. Robert Venturi and Denise Scott Brown, together with their associate Steven Izenour, followed this in 1972 with their treatise on 'Learning from Las Vegas'.

In 1991 Robert Venturi joined a very select band of recipients of the Pritzker Architecture Prize. The jury said 'He has expanded and redefined the limits of the art of architecture in this century, as perhaps no other has, through his theories and built works.'

Venturi Scott Brown and Associate's office is located in Main Street, Philadelphia, which perhaps suggests a tastefully restored Georgian house in the historic quarter near William Penn's original landing place. Not so, nor is it even in the centre of the modern city now some sixteen blocks back from the Delaware River. In fact it is several miles away in an old warehouse on the Schuylkill River in the charming and unspoilt little district of Manayunk. Somehow this seems to symbolize the slightly wistful humour and subtle wit which is the Venturis' trademark.

The practice is currently about 40 strong although it has been over twice that size in the recent past when several major projects were simultaneously live in the office. In addition to the two titular principals there are a number of associates, including Steven Izenour, one of the co-authors of *Learning from Las Vegas*. On the whole, Denise Scott Brown is more often the principal in charge of the larger-scale planning and urban design work while Robert Venturi is in charge of the architectural projects. However, they work closely together and the practice is clearly an integrated one. They have abandoned the idea of the more corporate structure which the practice had recently, with another partner taking more responsibility for management. While they do not necessarily enjoy having to do more management, Robert Venturi and Denise Scott Brown are 'much happier managing our own show' and feel that this extends to the staff generally. There is now the view that 'one person cannot do all the management that is needed in the firm'. Rather, this function is more widely spread and Denise Scott Brown has identified three levels of management which she calls X, Y and Z:[1]

The X is discrete tasks that people can handle, even young people, like maintaining the library and things like that. The Y are more interconnected tasks and are mostly in the charge of our associates and even lots of hiring, for example, is done by our associates. The Z are the high-level management tasks such as deciding how much marketing we will do or which jobs we should take, which Bob and I have to do advised by a small group of our senior associates.

Although they are well known as theoreticians Robert Venturi and Denise Scott Brown argue that theory should not dominate the design process. In fact Robert Venturi argues strongly that 'the artist is not someone who designs in order to prove his or her theory, and certainly not to suit an ideology'.[2] ... 'Any building that tries merely to express a theory or any building that starts with a theory and works very deductively is very dry, so we say that we work inductively.'

This is illustrated by their joint work *Learning from Las Vegas*. They argue that when they went to Las Vegas they had not so much a theory but more of a strong feeling and reaction to the place. They were asked what they had learnt from Las Vegas and initially used to reply that they could not say, but that this would show in their work. Eventually, of course, they wrote their famous book explaining the lessons about symbolism which they drew from the experience, enabling them to re-analyse history from a new point of view. Robert Venturi describes this process as 'the artist monitoring his reactions', and feels that the difficulty for many young artists is properly to monitor their intuitions.

They both feel that designers should be prepared to learn more by copying from the masters, and complain that, in recent years, students have been taught not to copy. Paradoxically, Denise Scott Brown points out that they copy ideologies. Robert Venturi summarizes this view with his saying that 'it is better to be good than to be original':[3]

[1] Office size and structure
This view of the need for the named principals of the practice to be heavily involved in the management of the practice is similar to that expressed by Ken Yeang. However, the identification of which tasks can be devolved to which levels of staff in the office seems special to the Venturis.

[2] Guiding principles
It is particularly interesting to see that such leading theoreticians feel this way about the relationship between theory and practice. The idea that a design should not be seen as a demonstration of a theory but rather a way of developing the theory shares some territory with Donald Schon's concept of the 'reflective practitioner'. The idea that practice is a way of exploring and developing theory is greatly strengthened by this contribution.

[3] Originality
Herman Hertzberger also points out that we seem to have been in an era during which originality has been valued for its own sake. Both Venturi and Hertzberger are asking us to question the validity of this when applied to design.

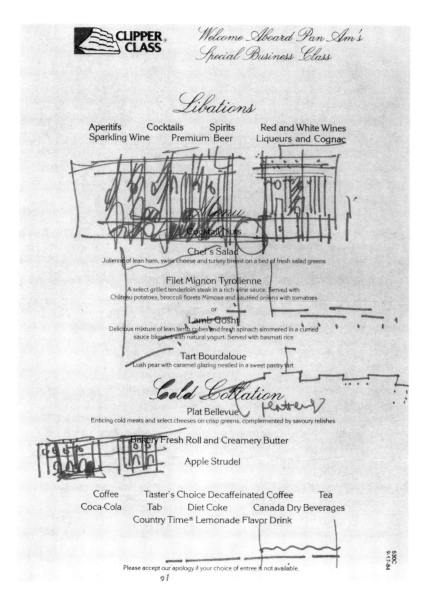

Here, material from the design process for the National Gallery extension in London is organized around the two themes of elevation and plan which can be seen as parallel lines of thought. Edward de Bono has published a complete book written on a long haul flight. Buildings take rather longer, but some of the basic ideas about the façade were already emerging, as can be seen from the subsequent sketches.

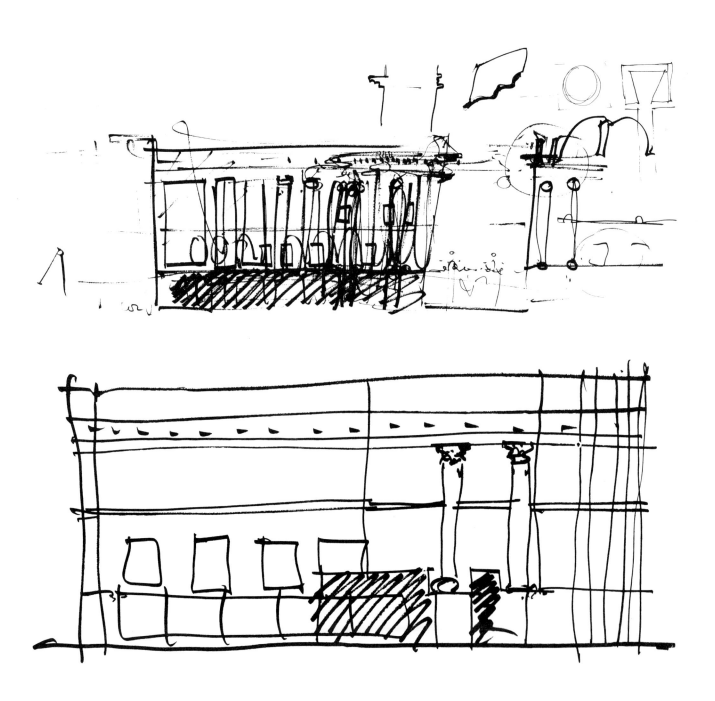

Sketches, models, collages, painting and computer generated images all play a role in the design process of Robert Venturi and Denise Scott Brown.

You have to have something basic that you either build on or evolve from or revolt against. You have to have something there in the first place and the only way to get it is to copy, in a good sense of the word.

Both acknowledge the central importance of drawing in their design process, but although many of Venturi's freehand sketches are highly expressive and beautiful in their own right, Denise Scott Brown is at pains to point out that 'these are never done as works of art but as communication with self'. They consider it essential for designers to have what Denise Scott Brown refers to as 'a facility between hand and mind', which she feels is 'Bob's great speciality'.[4] Sometimes the hand does something that the eye then re-interprets and you get an idea from it.

Computers are everywhere in the office, although the partners themselves tend to rely on their staff to operate them. They find that 'the people who can draw very well and who control line weight well in hand technique are the ones who use the computer imaginatively'. The partners are enthusiastic about the computer as a creative design tool not just as a drafting aid. In fact they claim they started to use a computer first as a design tool, using it for production drawings later. They like the facility the computer has for generating views and for geometric manipulation of elements.[5] 'The first thing we put on it was the columns from the [existing] National Gallery because we had to reproduce them so often at so many different scales.'

Denise Scott Brown talks of 'Bob sitting at the computer and getting out of it what he needs', which indicates a recognition that the computer must be put in its place among all the other tools available to the designer. In fact the Venturi's drawing office reveals considerable evidence of a plurality of communication techniques with models, hand drawings, paintings and collages as well as computer-generated images, and even full-size mock-ups. These items are deliberately left around not just in the studios but also in meeting rooms and offices. Robert Venturi believes that even when talking 'you suddenly see something else out of the corner of your eye and you think of something you wouldn't have done otherwise'. He believes that ideas come to him in a wide variety of ways, and certainly does not retreat to a quiet location to think. Sometimes ideas will come quickly and easily while on other projects 'the idea only comes after great struggle and agony':

The main idea for the National Gallery facade, for instance, came on the second day I was thinking about it in London. I was standing there in Trafalgar Square and it came like that, and it has lasted, although it took many months to refine it.

Alongside the plurality of images in the office, and their renowned 'learning from' places and history, Robert Venturi and Denise Scott Brown both find analogy a useful way of generating and describing design ideas.[6] Denise Scott Brown, for example, feels that the back of the National Gallery is very plain in the same way that 'you don't have lapels on the back of your suit':

[4] Drawing
Robert Venturi's views about drawing as part of the design process are very similar to those expressed by Herman Hertzberger and Richard Burton. The refusal to see drawings done during the design process as works of art is similar to the view expressed by Santiago Calatrava.

[5] Computer-aided design
This is one of the most sympathetic views about CAD as a design as opposed to the purely drafting tool that we have seen. The enthusiastic but pragmatic understanding of what the computer is or is not good at is very similar to that expressed by Ian Ritchie.

[6] Generation of ideas
The Venturis frequently emphasize the importance of analogy in their work. Not only do they enjoy making art which plays with analogues but they also see it as a vital tool in the creative and imaginative process. In this sense the wide variation of work in the office ranging from planning to product design and including both design and written theory suggests that they feed off this variety intellectually. They seem to share with Santiago Calatrava this apparent joy at working at so many different scales and using this as a creative stimulus.

'The main idea for the National Gallery façade came on the second day when I was standing in Trafalgar Square . . . it has lasted, although it took many months to refine it.' (Robert Venturi).

Analogy is there all the time in our thinking, and historical analogy is very important ... Bob is quite likely to say something like 'this fountain should be like an Edwardian lady's hat'.[7]

One of the inevitable consequences of a successful and busy practice without a separate management department, you would think, is that the design partners do less drawing and actual design work of their own, but this is not so: the consequence is that they work seven days a week. Their roles, Robert Venturi has said only somewhat facetiously, are those of manager, accountant, salesperson, lawyer, psychiatrist, actor and socialite, as well as artist. Of course, they depend upon the quality and expertise of their associates and staff and on the philosophic and artistic principles they all share. These translate project designs faithfully into reality, through design processes which are led and supervised by Robert Venturi and Denise Scott Brown from start to finish but which must, to some extent, rely on delegation followed by criticism:[8]

We have people who are extremely good and well trained so that it is possible now to get all their drawings up on this wall here and sit and critique them and draw on them ... it is a kind of guidance but that is only after some very basic things have been worked out ... We really direct people from the beginning.

Their view about the generation of alternatives is a subtle one, with more emphasis on this at the planning end of their work than with architecture:

The use of options in planning is to achieve democracy in the process. You have to accommodate more complexity and confront more political options in planning than in architecture[9]

Robert Venturi lays emphasis on a design process that works from the particular to the general as much as the other way round. The question of the resolution of detail seems to be a matter very close to Robert Venturi's heart. He believes this to be an integral part of the design process and likes to make the distinction between 'invention' and 'refinement'. For Venturi 'invention' involves originality and the 'what', whereas 'refinement' involves development and the 'how'. He considers both of equal importance in the creative process and he and Denise Scott Brown believe in doing both together in order to achieve real quality in design. He feels that recently invention has been encouraged at the expense of refinement, resulting in a consequent loss of quality in design. Robert Venturi greatly regrets the increasing tendency in the United States to separate conceptual design from design development, which he argues must be detrimental to quality in design:

We have a rule that says sometimes the detail wags the dog. You don't necessarily go from the general to the particular, but rather often you do detailing at the beginning very much to inform.[10]

[7]**Images**
This use of images seems very similar to that employed by Richard MacCormac. Of course, images can be dangerous and misleading as well as powerful. This sort of image seems to offer the useful characteristic of being non-visually expressed shorthand which can be used to share a design concept before it can be realized. A particular advantage early in the process is that a verbally expressed image does not draw attention to extraneous detail which may detract from the central idea of the argument. See also the way Eva Jiricna likes to express ideas in words in discussion with her clients before exchanging any visual communication.

[8]**Intervention**
This represents a system in which members of the design team are given considerable responsibility, but within the context of project designs created by Robert Venturi and Denise Scott Brown and controlled by them through all details. Ongoing work on projects is supervised by interventions which are like design school criticism sessions, but only after specific on-the-drawing-board directives have been given. However, the whole process is conducted in relation to clearly shared views about the guiding principles of the practice, which have been made explicit through the extensive range of publications by Robert Venturi and Denise Scott Brown. This then presents a situation rather similar to that seen in the practices of Ken Yeang and John Outram.

[9]**Alternatives**
This is an interesting view about the generation of alternatives in design. By contrast, Eva Jiricna who works at the scale of interior design for individual clients, likes to generate many alternatives. Thus in spite of Denise Scott Brown's argument about the difference between architecture and planning, it seems more likely that this is in fact a highly personal matter.

[10]**Detail**
This is a very similar argument about detailed design helping to resolve the main concepts or central ideas as those advanced by Richard MacCormac. Probably, though, Eva Jiricna follows the most extreme version of this approach to design through detail.

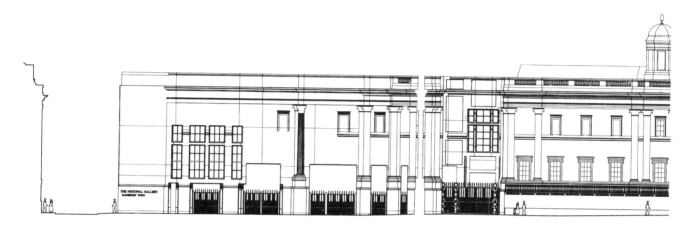

EXTENDED SOUTH ELEVATION
THE NATIONAL GALLERY SAINSBURY WING
TRAFALGAR SQUARE   LONDON
VENTURI, SCOTT BROWN AND ASSOCIATES

'The main idea for the National Gallery façade came on the second day when I was standing in Trafalgar Square . . . it has lasted, although it took many months to refine it.' (Robert Venturi).

Robert Venturi recognizes that, like many designers, he is inclined to 'jump in before you know everything ... and have the design inform the programme'. However, even though he is a distinguished theoretician, Robert Venturi does not enjoy designing in the abstract, preferring to confront what he refers to as 'reality' early in the process.[11] 'I do not resist facing reality very early ... I love facing the reality of the budget and so on.' However, he also makes an interesting point about oscillating during his design process between the theoretical and the practical:

What you do very often is you face the reality for certain moments and then you say 'to heck with the reality' and you do the fantastic and you go back and forth ... but in this episodic process there must be a loving of the reality. When you get to the reality phase you don't resist it or resent it ... within reason, naturally, if your budget is absurd or utterly perverse then you do resent it, but the reality is the fun part of it. I love facing reasonably nasty reality.

Robert Venturi is quite clear that during the early phases of his design process he may have several ideas developing in parallel which may not be resolved. A good example of this would be the way he developed his ideas about the facade of the National Gallery's Sainsbury Wing, as well as having ideas about access and about continuing the axis internally from the existing building. Only later were all these resolved into a single solution.[12]

Robert Venturi and Denise Scott Brown are generally unenthusiastic about design competitions, and used to refuse to enter them, although some of their most well-known recent work has come from competitions.[13] 'We think that architecture has to derive from collaboration ... and we learn a lot from the client ... we get some of our best ideas from clients, we love collaborating with them.'

They emphasize the need for trust between architect and client to get the best out of their process. Denise Scott Brown talks about the 'client letting you be on their side', which seems to come at least in part from their experience of working for committees rather than individual clients. Robert Venturi describes the need 'not to worry about saying something stupid'.[14] ... 'You need sometimes to think out loud and be free to say stupid things ... and if the client has faith this can often lead to something.'

Robert Venturi stresses the critical importance of the skill of criticism and what he calls 'editing' as part of the design process. Denise Scott Brown refers to this as 'the judgement to winnow' which she thinks is one of Venturi's particular skills. 'Everyone can have bright ideas, but it is the ability to say this one is less pertinent, that one is more pertinent so let's start and build here.'

There may be some debate on the part of observers and critics as to whether Robert Venturi invented 'Post-modernism'. While there can be no doubt that he has been responsible for moving architecture on from the Modern Movement both as a practitioner and as a theorist, he 'objects to being called a Post-modernist because we don't like being associated with so much bad art'. Both Robert Venturi and Denise Scott Brown are suspicious of designers who invent names for their styles which they consider more for the historians. 'Bernini didn't know he was Baroque ... Freud was not a Freudian and Marx was not a Marxist.'

Robert Venturi is not sympathetic to the use of technology as a generative force in architectural design and he argues against the idea that a building needs to be technologically advanced.[15]

[11] **Reality and innovation**
A similar dislike of designing in the abstract was expressed by Santiago Calatrava. This seems to represent a view held strongly by some designers that they are at their most creative when faced with real rather than abstract problems. Ken Yeang also makes a similar point about the need to see the budget as a positive rather than a negative feature of the problem.

[12] **Parallel lines of thought**
This is a very good example of a designer having apparently disconnected ideas about the solution which are allowed to co-exist in the mind early in the process without feeling the need to resolve conflicts which they may generate. Of course, these ideas about plan and facade which appear in this particular example would have been extremely difficult to hold while conforming to the principles of the Modern Movement. This indicates an important but largely unexplored issue concerning the relationship between the design process and the designer's philosophy of design. Much of the literature on the design process has tended implicitly to assume that process and style are independent, and that findings about the process hold true, irrespective of periods of stylistic or philosophic change. Clearly this is not so.

[13] **Competitions**
This is a fairly common view of architectural design competitions, but see the chapter on Herman Hertzberger for a particularly similar criticism. Certainly one of the most frequently expressed views in this book is the central importance of the client in the design process. This must be missing in the competition.

[14] **Trust and the client**
Herman Hertzberger made very similar comments about the need for the client to trust the architect.

[15] **Technology**
Robert Venturi seems close to Michael Wilford's view of technology as a second- or even third-level consideration. The subsequent argument that the expression of technology should be related to the wider context of technology in society is also similar to John Outram's view. The idea, however, that today's technology is electronic raises some fascinating possibilities for the architecture of the age of virtual reality.

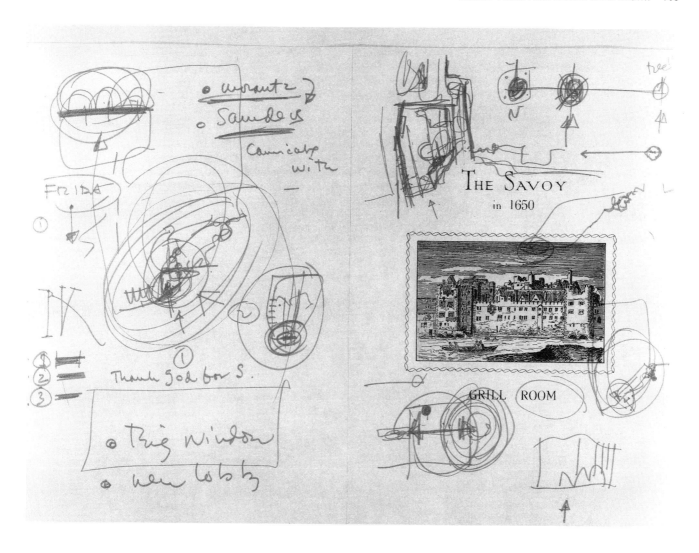

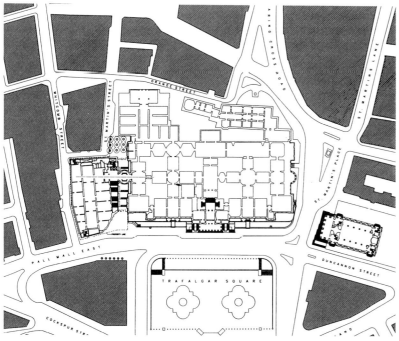

The beginning and end of the second line of thought, about the plan. The inventor Rowland Emett has said that although inventors are supposed to sketch their ideas on the back of an envelope, he prefers to use the front so he can include the stamp and the design is already half done!

I think that it is generally a good idea to be conservative ... an awful lot of good architecture is reliant on quite a slow evolution of technology, unlike a car, a building has to last a hundred years ... The technology that is exciting today is computers, it's electronic technology and that is not visible.

He also points out that building and civil engineering technology are not really symbolic of our time as might have been the case at the end of the nineteenth century, when great advances were being made in new materials and techniques. Of course, Robert Venturi's attitude towards the 'Post-modern' leaves him unsympathetic to the dominating form generating notion of structural honesty. Denise Scott Brown explains this possible disjunction between form and technology by introducing the concept of symbol with which the Venturis have been so strongly associated.[16] 'We say form follows function, but symbol does not [necessarily] follow function.'

Robert Venturi also argues that architects should make a distinction between civic art and more private buildings. He accepts that 'often advanced and original art is considered outrageous at the time', and worries that this idea has been translated in recent times into a feeling that something cannot be considered of value unless it is esoteric. However, he argues there has been a long tradition of 'civic art being agreeable to the masses', and considers that 'esoteric civic art is an oxymoron'.

[16]**Symbol**
With tongue in cheek the Venturis also like to describe their own obviously symbiotic relationship by describing themselves as 'Mr Form and Mrs Function'.

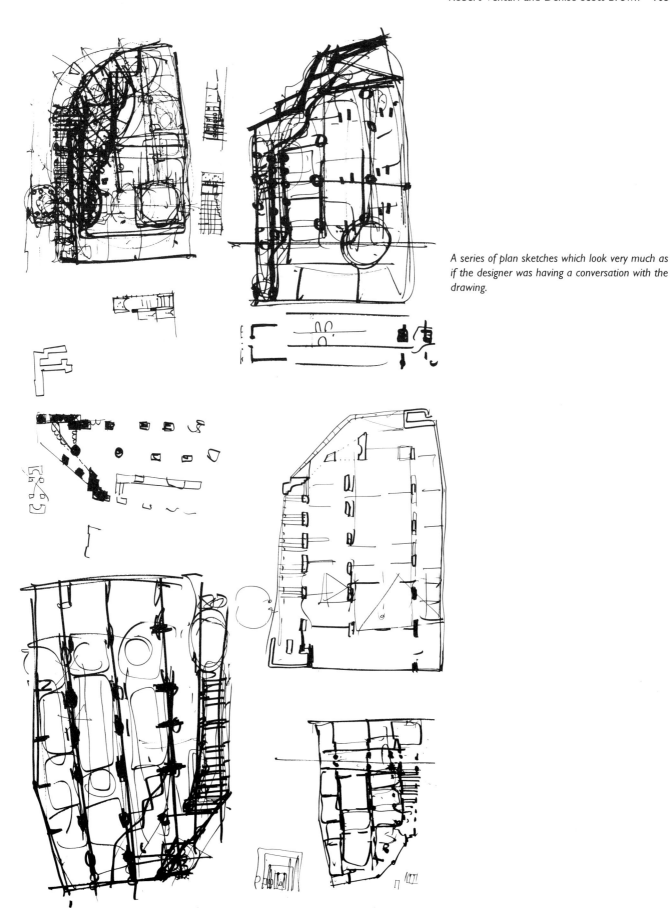

A series of plan sketches which look very much as if the designer was having a conversation with the drawing.

Robert Venturi and Denise Scott Brown

Bibliography

Jenkins, D. (1991). Capital gains. *Architects' Journal*, **21/28** August, 22–33.

Maxwell, R. (1991). Both serious and popular. *Architecture Today*, **20**, 30–41.

Ostler, T. (1991). First past the post. *Building Design*, 13 December, 12–14.

Papadakis, A. C. (ed.). (1992). *Venturi Scott Brown and Associates: On Houses and Housing*, London: Academy Editions.

Schwartz, F. (ed.). (1992). *Mother's House: the evolution of Vanna Venturi's house in Chestnut Hill*, New York: Rizzoli.

Scott Brown, D. (1969). On pop art, permissiveness and planning. *Journal of the American Institute of Planners*, **XXXV**(3), 184–186.

Scott Brown, D. (1990). *Urban Concepts*, London: Academy Editions.

Venturi, D., and Scott Brown, D. (1991). Architecture as elemental shelter, the city as valid decon. *Architectural Design*, **61**(11/12), 8–13.

Venturi, R. (1966, revised edition 1977). *Complexity and Contradiction in Architecture*, New York: The Museum of Modern Art.

Venturi, R. (1981). The RIBA Annual Discourse. *RIBA Journal*, May, 47–56.

Venturi, R., Scott Brown, D. and Izenour, S. (1972, revised edition 1977). *Learning from Las Vegas: the forgotten symbolism of architectural form*, Cambridge, Mass.: MIT Press.

Michael Wilford

Michael Wilford was born in Surrey and studied architecture at the North London Polytechnic, graduating with distinction in 1962. Even before completing his studies, and as early as 1960, he was working for James Stirling and James Gowan. That partnership broke up in 1963 and Michael Wilford became an Associate Partner with James Stirling in 1965. Michael Wilford also studied at the Regent Street Polytechnic Planning School in London, and much of his work since has been at the scale of urban design. The practice of James Stirling, Michael Wilford and Associates was formed in 1971, and the association between James Stirling and Michael Wilford thus represents one of the longest-running periods of sustained cooperation at this level of design. Sadly, this was terminated by the untimely death of James Stirling in 1992, during the preparation of this book. The new practice of Michael Wilford and Partners incorporates the previous practice of James Stirling, Michael Wilford and Associates. They have offices in London, Singapore and Stuttgart.

The work of Stirling and Wilford is well known around the world, although they have built surprisingly little in their home country. Their best known and most successful work has been for institutions such as universities, museums and art galleries, where they have frequently been able to contribute to the public domain. They have built on both sides of the Atlantic and most recently Michael Wilford has been working on a complete polytechnic in Singapore, which represents one of the largest jobs ever to pass through the practice.

Michael Wilford has also been heavily involved in education and has lectured and examined widely. He has taught at schools of architecture in the USA, Canada, Britain and Australia, and has held visiting professorships in both the USA and the UK. He has received an honorary doctorate from the University of Sheffield, with which he has had a long association.

Innocent passers-by in a central London square would be unlikely to be aware of their proximity to one of the world's most renowned architects, for James Stirling, Michael Wilford and Associates do little to advertise the presence of their office. However, once through the elegant facade the visitor almost instantly and somewhat surprisingly penetrates what in most offices would be the inner sanctum. Michael Wilford's own room on the first floor is separated from his secretaries only by large open doors. He refers to this as the engine room of the office symbolically occupying the central floor of the building with two more storeys above and two below. It is also highly significant that, until the sudden death of James Stirling, Michael and Jim shared this room since they operated quite literally as a partnership. Work was not divided vertically between the partners and down through the office, as often happens in such practices. While it was inevitably the case that one partner or the other took the lead in each job, both were involved in all the work. Both of them could see all the mail, whether ingoing or outgoing, and obviously overhear each other's conversations, thus allowing them to make their contributions as they felt necessary.

The practice is quite small, with under 30 core staff, and ultimately limited in size by this personal approach.[1] They have often operated by working with other practices on their overseas jobs, sometimes opening a satellite office for the duration of the larger projects. While Michael Wilford tends to make the client presentations, each job will be assigned to an associate as project architect who will be responsible for all stages of the project. Ideas come from the project team as well as from the partners, and the team grows in size as the project progresses. Michael Wilford draws a parallel between the way they work and that of a newspaper office:

The process is just like a newspaper editor who will take copy and say 'well I think the slant of this is kind of wrong, I think you have not covered this aspect of it, let's focus here, let's balance this, let's re-do it, I don't like this'. So it's very much this kind of process and in the end the design has that kind of personal touch, that slant if you like of the editor in its final form. But the generation of the idea is not always the editor's, it's the result of a labyrinth of ideas that develop in the office and somehow come together and get ordered, sifted, and prioritized.[2]

Michael Wilford considers the relationship with the client to be worth considerable care and attention. He believes that Stirling and Wilford's 'best work has been done when a client comes to us who knows us already and he'll come to us and say "I want you to do a building"'. This attitude leads them not to do competitions unless they are invited and paid. Michael Wilford believes at least this commitment by the client is necessary before engaging in a project. In fact Michael Wilford sees the client as having a key role in the design process:[3]

Behind every building of distinction is an equally distinctive client, not necessarily high profile, but one who takes the time and trouble to comprehend the ideas of the architect, is supportive and enthusiastic, who is bold, willing to take risks and, above all, can hold his or her nerve during the inevitable crises.

Much of Stirling and Wilford's work concerns large public buildings and thus they have tended to find themselves briefed by client committees. Michael Wilford sees the importance of identifying those members of the committee who are really committed to producing good architecture.

---

[1]Office size and structure
It is interesting to compare this organization with that of the other partnership practices in this study. Ahrends, Burton and Koralek, for example, seem much more clearly divided almost into three practices. However, it is worth noting that the way they worked when smaller and in their earlier days is similar to the organization described here by Michael Wilford.

[2]Intervention
Michael Wilford is almost playing down his role as a generator of design ideas here in a way that is quite difficult to believe when looking at the strongly coherent body of work to emerge from Stirling and Wilford. However, we can certainly take this to mean that he tries to encourage ideas to emerge upwards as much as downwards in the design team. Clearly junior staff are not just expected to work up the ideas handed down from the top. By contrast, for example, both Santiago Calatrava and Herman Hertzberger appear to take much more of a leadership role than this editorial metaphor suggests that Michael Wilford intends.

[3]Role of the client
The importance of the client's role is emphasized by so many of the contributors to this book. However, Michael Wilford's comments on this matter correspond most closely with those of Richard Burton. This also seems a similar view to that reflected by the way Denise Scott Brown and Robert Venturi talk of how 'we love to collaborate with them [clients]'.

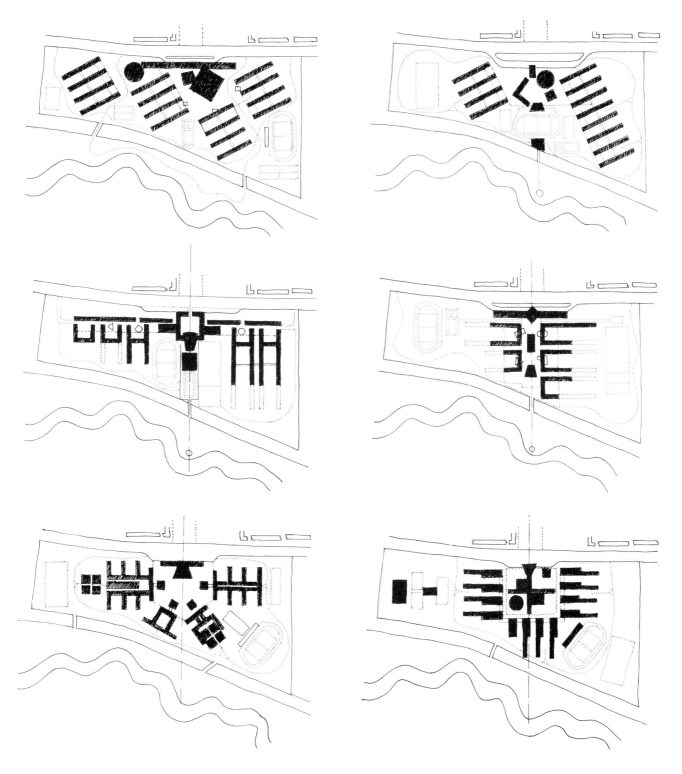

Michael Wilford describes a design process which includes the generation of many alternatives. Here we see a number, although not all, of the alternative site layouts considered for Temasek Polytechnic in Singapore.

Sometimes such members may leave the committee during the course of the project for some reason, and Michael Wilford feels that this can have a significant effect on the job. 'As a result of that you can sense the project languishing and on the back burner with nobody agitating it.'[4] Michael Wilford believes in taking the client through a very carefully ordered and structured process in which both brief and design develop together:

We have found over the years that the ideal brief is probably one or two pages even for the most complex project. Many clients think they have got to produce something that is two inches thick before an architect can even put pen to paper. We prefer it the other way round, we prefer the thinnest possible information so that we can get a grasp on the whole thing and then gradually embellish it with detail later.

Michael Wilford likes to see the site and basic accommodation requirements drawn to the same scale on sheets of paper no larger than A3 or A4:

I like to see things encapsulated in one small image. We have a rule never to draw at a size larger than necessary to convey the level of information intended ... we always use the smallest possible image.

Working with this fairly minimal brief and using the same graphical format, the project team will develop a series of as many alternative ideas as possible.[5] These are then discussed with the partners and gradually a few design strategies are identified which are seen to have 'validity and architectural potential'. The production of a range of alternatives is one of the keys to the way Stirling and Wilford interact with their clients. However, from his experience as a teacher Michael Wilford finds that design students often do not have the ability to produce a range of alternative ideas. 'They can't detach themselves from a particular solution or design to look at others.' In this situation Michael Wilford feels

they are locked into a solution without having a full spectrum available to judge whether that is an appropriate solution. Without this the process tends to become ephemeral, whereas I think it needs to be rooted in a very systematic process of investigation of options and selection.[6]

Stirling and Wilford involve the client in this process, with the appropriate partner taking perhaps three or four ideas for joint discussions. Michael Wilford believes these discussions have two-way benefits. First it enables him better to understand what the client really wants, what is critical, what is important, and what is optional. Second it also commits the client to supporting the principles on which the design is based. 'Right from the beginning the client has an involvement and not only does he end up with a schematic design that he's contributed to, because we use him as part of the editorial role I was describing, but because he's been part of the process, the client is committed to it.'

The proven success of this technique is, however, quite clearly dependent at least to some extent upon the nature of the alternatives presented. Here Michael Wilford emphasizes the importance of keeping to basic diagrammatic drawings which show organization and massing but not style or appearance

We actually make it clear that these diagrams are totally abstract ... actually this is one of the frustrations that some clients have with us ... we have a long talk at

[4] The committee client
What Michael Wilford is drawing our attention to here is the skill needed to manage a client represented not by an individual but by a committee. These skills seem different to those needed to manage the individual client with whom the designer can have a personal relationship. For similar thoughts on the committee client see the chapter on Richard Burton, while that on Eva Jiricna probably represents the ultimate in the careful and thoughtful management of the relationship with an individual client.

[5] Drawing
We can see several other very similar attitudes towards this use of quite small images in the work of Santiago Calatrava and Herman Hertzberger. The idea of concentrating on an image that can be taken in without having to move the head or scan the eyes across large sheets seems quite important to all these designers.

[6] Alternatives
Both Eva Jiricna and Richard Burton also describe a process explicitly based on the generation of alternatives and then selecting from them. However, as can be seen from a study of those two chapters and this, the way these alternatives are generated varies considerably between these three designers.

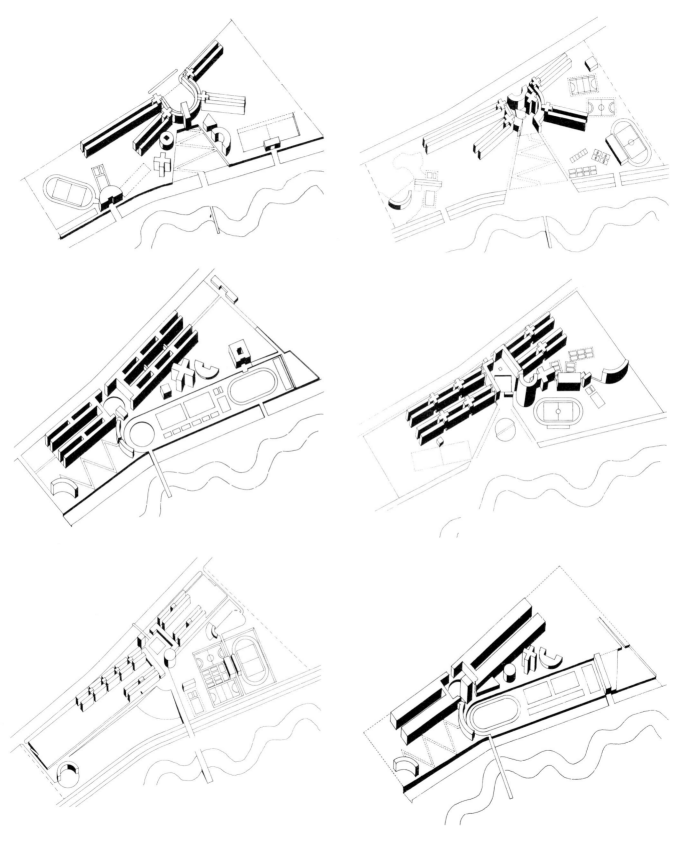

More alternatives for the same site in the form of three-dimensional images which show the massing of the buildings without any detail.

the beginning of this process and say to them 'you're not going to see what this building is going to look like for several months'.[7]

This is not a process of concealing the appearance of the scheme from the client, since the architects themselves are focusing on other issues. Michael Wilford offers an extremely practical almost prosaic account of this process. For him, matters will automatically be resolved at what he considers to be the right time as a result of keeping strictly to his view of priorities. 'It's just a matter of sequence ... I think the skill is prioritizing the stages at which certain inputs are valuable as distinct from an impediment to the process.' Michael Wilford realizes that all this can sound a little simplistic, but he emphasizes the importance of experience here in controlling the way other influences are gradually brought into this process

One is bringing to bear an unconscious body of attitudes and experience in that decision-making process. I can make it sound very pragmatic, and actually it is, but the pragmatics are guided or conditioned by this other layer of concern in the subconscious that is very difficult to articulate.

For Michael Wilford the early generators of design ideas are very much to do with the function of the building

One of the things that is absolutely fundamental to us is that the buildings are functional ... in other words, that they do the things the client wants ... we have absolutely no interest in forcing architectural solutions onto clients that are inappropriate to their needs.

This early phase of design, then, is one in which Stirling and Wilford avoid the emotive issues to do with the appearance of their architecture in order fully to expand their slim brief to understand the client's functional needs in detail. 'We go through a fairly long methodical process to draw them out on this.'[8]

Michael Wilford is not particularly enthusiastic about modern technology in the design office. He tends to sing the praises of basic facilities like the Xerox machine rather than more advanced technology. The practice has only relatively recently started to use word processors and might soon install desktop publishing facilities. Michael Wilford does not anticipate using computer-aided design, although he sees the benefits of computer-aided drafting as a labour-saving and coordinating tool

I think really for us the process of designing is working with paper and pencils, it's a reiterative and comparative process ... I just cannot conceive of why one would want to detach oneself from the very immediate process of drawing lines on paper and tracing through.[9]

Michael Wilford feels that after several years of experience an architect begins to work intuitively:

All the time one is making decisions about the disposition of rooms and how they are organized, one is also checking with a series of three-dimensional drawings and so there are ideas and disciplines of the massing which are driving the design forward as well.

[7] **Relationship with the client**
It is worth noting how much emphasis Herman Hertzberger places on the level of trust needed between designer and client. Denise Scott Brown and Robert Venturi talk of the need for the client to 'let you be on their side'. Clearly for Michael Wilford's method to work there must be substantial trust, since the client is required to remain curious as to how the building will look for a considerable period of time. Eva Jiricna seems to be making a similar point when she describes verbally reaching agreement with the client before showing any drawings. We should remember here that Michael Wilford has already told us that Stirling and Wilford's best work is done when the client approaches them, and therefore presumably already has some expectancies about the kind of design which will eventually result. It remains an interesting question as to the extent to which this process could be made to work by designers with a lesser reputation.

[8] **Radical constraints as primary generators.**
Michael Wilford seems to be telling us that it is the very essence of the building type that gives him his starting point, or in the language of 'How Designers Think', that his primary generators tend to come from the radical constraints. However, as we shall see soon, the external constraints also figure strongly in Michael Wilford's early considerations.

[9] **Computer-aided design**
This is a similar, although perhaps more negative, view to that expressed by Herman Hertzberger on this issue. It contrasts most strongly with that of Ian Ritchie, who has demonstrated that a reiterative and comparative process can be supported by computers. More recently Michael Wilford's practice has begun to use a computer-aided drafting system.

One alternative worked up into considerably more detail.

He emphasizes the integrated nature of decision making at this stage, and uses the analogy of a

juggler who's got six balls in the air ... and an architect is similarly operating on at least six fronts simultaneously and if you take you eye off one of them and drop it, you're in trouble. There is a sequential development but it's on several fronts simultaneously.[10]

Clearly, contextualism is one of these major generating forces for Michael Wilford. He invariably describes the surroundings of his sites when asked to explain how a particular design developed. Many of Stirling and Wilford's recent projects have been on urban sites and this attention to the surrounding forms and materials is evident in the final designs. Perhaps this is most obviously developed in the Clore extension to the Tate Gallery, where the surface materials, colours and patterns within the scheme are used to create a most unusual transition between the buildings on either side. In their more recent work for a new polytechnic in Singapore the site is open and less urban, but Michael Wilford still talks of the surrounding roads, scale of buildings, adjacent lake and other natural features which have been used to generate aspects of the design.[11] By contrast, Michael Wilford feels strongly that technical factors should not normally have a major dominating influence in architectural design:

They are not primary generators of the architecture unless you are doing something like a sports stadium or a bridge. They are secondary, maybe even tertiary considerations. I think that the character of the building, the quality of the building derives from its spaces and its functions and social characteristics rather than its fancy structure or its external flexible air conditioning system, or its toilets, or its fire escape. I think there are much more significant aspects of architecture that should be used to convey a character than those technical elements.[12]

The architectural language that Stirling and Wilford use has been the subject of much analysis, but Michael Wilford is dismissive of some of the critics' attempts to categorize their work:

The issue of style is somewhat of a red herring. I think authenticity or integrity is what is really important. I mean so many of these buildings which have labels, stylistic labels are so shallow.

This attitude is perhaps best exemplified by Stirling and Wilford's a new architectural vocabulary. Michael Wilford frequently uses the word 'veneer' in conversation to describe the way they use many surface materials. This he sees as 'a straight technical response, it's a very pragmatic response to current circumstances ... it recognizes the current economic constraint and limitations on craftsmanship'. Michael Wilford argues that when you can only afford to use

marble which is 25–30 mm thick you actually design and detail accordingly ... that is not a problem, it doesn't detract from the merit of the material. In fact the open joints which are a consequence of supporting each of the stones in stainless steel cramps means that you can design that veneer to accept huge thermal fluctuations without problems of mastic breaking down or mortar popping out and you get a very strong shadow between stones.

[10]**Speed of working**
Richard MacCormac uses the same image of the designer as a juggler. Of course, a juggler is only seen to be clever because he must turn his attention so quickly from one item to another. Richard Burton makes a similar point about the need to alternate quickly over a wide range of issues. He, like Michael Wilford, finds this a skill which comes only with experience. Perhaps this is a lesson which should be learned by those who feel that design education takes too long. Of course, it is possible to study all the issues in a much shorter time than that needed to develop the skill to handle them like a juggler.

[11]**External constraints**
See the earlier note about Primary Generators. It seems that the context of the building and the basic functions of the building combine in Michael Wilford's eyes to make each project different, and it is from a study of these two that his early ideas primarily develop.

[12]**Technology**
This is quite a strong and clear statement about the role of technology, or practical constraints, in the design process, and seems to be shared by Robert Venturi. It might be contrasted, for example, with the views of Eva Jiricna, which seem almost diametrically opposed to those expressed here.

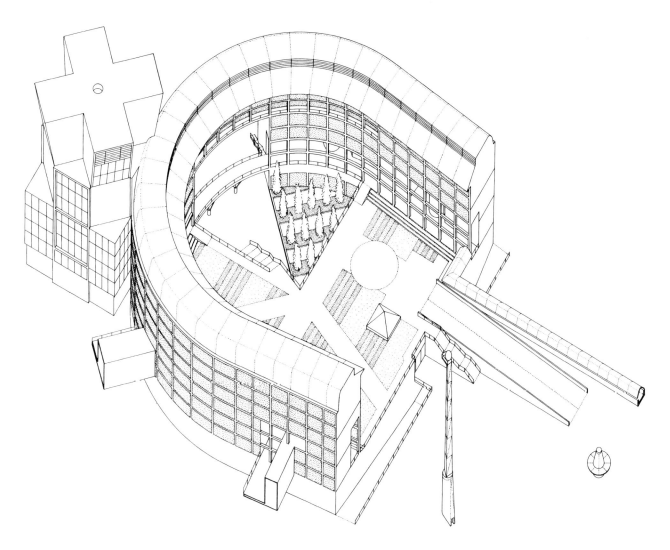

A part of the previous solution shown in detail. The actual appearance of the buildings becomes apparent.

This in turn appears to allow Stirling and Wilford to use their materials as veneers to create formal arrangements which would not be possible in traditional loadbearing construction without losing the integrity which Michael Wilford clearly uses as a major guiding principle.

Michael Wilford tries to create architecture which has meaning on several levels but without, as he puts it, 'getting over-philosophical'. 'I think that a building should be of sufficient interest that when you visit it for the third, fourth or fifth time you discover new things about it that weren't initially apparent like a series of layers that you can gradually work your way through … but I don't think you should have to read a book to understand it.' Michael Wilford believes in learning lessons from the past, and is critical of the way 'the Modern Movement erased everything', However, he denies an interest in style. 'In the sense the word is used, I think style implies superficiality and we don't think it's important and certainly not a generator.' In particular, he is not interested in applied symbolism but believes that a building should communicate its purpose through form rather than detail.[13]

Michael Wilford stresses a number of issues about his approach to the design process. He believes in beginning with an extensive investigation of the range of possible solutions to the functional problems. This process allows him to interact with the client in order more fully to understand the brief and also to commit the client to the generic solution before dealing with matters of appearance. He stresses the importance of judging just when in the process each issue should be considered, and through this the eventual solution emerges:

I think the skill is prioritizing, the stage at which certain inputs are valuable as distinct from an impediment to the process. So it goes back to this business of selecting and editing so that you have a clear idea of what you want to achieve in order to make that editing process meaningful.

[13]**Style**
Other designers in this book express a similar disinterest in style, and one senses a slight resentment at the way critics classify their work in stylistic terms. Eva Jiricna and Ian Ritchie, in particular, talk in a way similar to Michael Wilford about the integrity of their work being of more importance to them than some supposed consistency of style. Robert Venturi's comment that 'Bernini didn't know he was Baroque' seems to make a similar point.

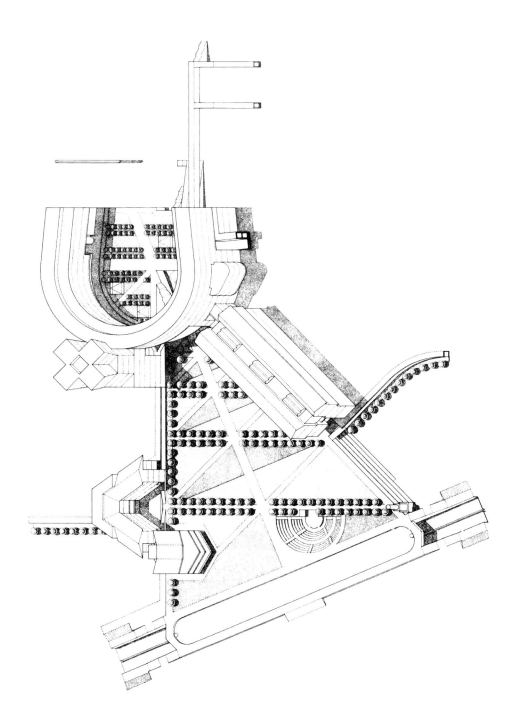

Michael Wilford

Bibliography

Arnell, P., and Bickford, T. (eds) (1984). *James Stirling, Michael Wilford and Associates: buildings and projects*, London: The Architectural Press.

Buchanan, P. (1988). Tate on the Mersey. *Architectural Review*, **184**(1097), 18–27.

Colquhoun, A. (1984). Democratic monument. *Architectural Review*, **176**(1054), 19–22.

Dennis, M., and Stirling, J. (1986). Sackler sequence. *Architectural Review*, **180**(1073), 26–33.

Jenks, C. (1987). Post-modernism and discontinuity. *Architectural Design*, **57**(1/2), 5–8.

Jenks, C., and Stirling, J. (1987). Clore contextualisms. *Architectural Review*, **181**(1084), 47–50.

Maxwell, R. (1989). Compact at Ithica. *Architectural Review*, **185**(1113), 36–49.

Maxwell, R. (1990). The surprising future: Stirling's return to Stuttgart. *Architecture Today*, **13**(36–45).

Stirling, J., and Wilford, M. (1984). *James Stirling, Buildings and Projects*. New York: Rizzoli.

Stirling, J., and Wilford, M. (1990). Music school/theatre academy and new civic square in Stuttgart. *Architecture Today*, **13**, 46–55.

Stirling, J., and Wilford, M. (1990). James Stirling, Michael Wilford and Associates: An architectural design profile. *Architectural Design*, **60**(5–6), complete special issue.

Summerson, J. (1987). Vitruvius ridens or laughter at the Tate. *Architectural Review*, **181**(1084), 45–46.

Wates, N. (1993). Michael Wilford: Looking to the future. *RIBA Journal*, **100**(3), 24–28.

Weston, R., and Januszcak, W. (1988). Stirling statement. *Architects' Journal*, **187**(27), 32–49.

Wilford, M. (1991). Inspired patronage. *RIBA Journal*, **98**(4), 36–42.

Wilford, M. (1991). A civic presence for a garden city. *Architecture Today*, **21**, 24–29.

Ken Yeang

Ken Yeang was born on the beautiful Malaysian island of Penang in 1948. He received part of his education at Cheltenham College in England and eventually studied at the Architectural Association, where he graduated in 1972. From there he went to the Department of Landscape Architecture at the University of Pennsylvania in the United States, where he studied with Ian Mcharg. He formed a partnership with Tengku Robert Hamzah of the Kelantan Royal Family with whom he has been in practice since 1976 with offices both in his native Penang and in the capital of Malaysia, Kuala Lumpur. His studies, however, had still not finished for, in 1981 he received his doctorate from Cambridge University, which was concerned with the role of ecological considerations in the design of the built environment.

Ken Yeang has maintained his interest in ecology and has applied this to his practice in the tropical climate so characteristic of the South-east Asian region. The practice of T. R. Hamzah and Yeang has won awards for its work at the scales of interior, building and urban design. In particular, they have developed a reputation for designing climatically responsive tall buildings. Dr Yeang himself has also continued to write and lecture on his search for a new form of architectural expression which both has a regional identity and is ecologically sound. He has published a whole string of influential articles in both Asian and European journals. Ken Yeang is the author of several books and has also had books published about his work.

Ken Yeang has taught and examined at the Universiti Teknologi Malaysia and at the Institute Teknologi Malaysia, as well at other schools of architecture in Europe, the United States of America and Asia. He has served as a member of both the Malaysian Government Boards of Architects and Engineers. Ken Yeang has been Vice-President of the Commonwealth Association of Architects, and Chairman of the Architects Regional Council of Asia (ARCASIA). In 1983 he was elected as President of Pertubuhan Arkitek Malaysia (The Malaysian Institute of Architects).

The office of T. R. Hamzah and Yeang is in one of the suburbs of Kuala Lumpur, the capital of Malaysia. Most of their work is in the same city, always posing the problem of building in a hot and humid tropical climate and frequently on restricted urban sites. A great deal of their work is commissioned by commercial clients and mostly built on a speculative basis. The office has, like many others, varied in size over its life but is now about 60 strong, with a high proportion of young, newly qualified staff and students.

Ken Yeang himself is something of a polymath and has described himself as 'an architectural kleptomaniac'. Although he qualified first as an architect he subsequently studied biology, bionics and ecology, and he now also takes an active interest in the theories of management and marketing. This varied background, itself a result of his naturally inquisitive mind, makes him a challenging conversationalist, with no topic safe from attack by him on several fronts.

Ken Yeang and his partner Tengku Robert Hamzah take an interest in and monitor all projects but delegate each one to a design architect who can become the project architect as the job progresses with a team growing and shrinking in size as appropriate. All projects are assigned to a 'design architect' and a 'job architect'.[1] Ken Yeang easily rehearses his view of the way responsibilities are distributed within the office which clearly grow out of his considerable study of management and business principles. First he is quick to point out that the responsibilities at his level include running the practice as a business:

We must see the practice as a business, the business has to make a profit, the business has to have a future, the business has to grow and be successfully marketed and developed. There are three things an architect has to do and if he does not do any of these three well he will be out on the streets. He has to get the business, he has to run the business and he has to do the business. I have to proportion my time between these three things.

For Ken Yeang, then, design has to be seen as an activity which should not be thought of in isolation, and can only be meaningfully studied in the context of this management structure

The secret of being a successful professional consultant, whether doctor, accountant or architect, is knowing where and when to devote exceptional personal attention. You can't put your hands on too many things, you have to delegate but knowing when to put your hands on at the right time and for how long is the secret of the successful professional.

Ken Yeang feels that the corporate approach, where a different person handles separate management functions, does not work for architects:

Clients don't like it, clients come to you and like you to be entirely responsible ... this is what makes our profession so stressful, you must have multiple management functions. I have to handle design, production, marketing, management and financial controls. I have to do all these because this is what our clients expect.[2]

Although predominantly working on commercial projects Ken Yeang demands that each project advances the practice's thinking about a continuing theoretical and investigative agenda of issues. This agenda originated from his early research work in Cambridge in the 1970s. The most

[1] Office size and structure
Compared with UK practice this seems rather large but the high proportion of newly qualified staff and students probably explains this. The formal organization of design architects and job architects also reflects perhaps a method of working which is culturally slightly different to that found in the United Kingdom, but is more like that of the USA.

[2] Design management
Ken Yeang sees the designer here very much as a professional consultant. Like doctors and lawyers, he feels that their clients demand personal attention and expect this integrated functionality. While some practices clearly work quite successfully using the corporate structure, Ken would probably agree that this is probably only possible where the marketplace has been educated to accept this kind of relationship. Many of our designers have referred to the importance of establishing trust between client and designer, and Ken Yeang seems to believe his office needs to be structured in this way in order to contribute to this process. It is interesting to relate these ideas to the arguments expressed by Denise Scott Brown and Robert Venturi about distributing management functions.

DESIGN PRINCIPLES & AGENDA

• Generally, the service-core position is of central importance in the design of the tall building. The service-core not only has structural ramifications, its location can affect the thermal performance of the building, its views and determines what parts of the peripheral walls will have openings and glazing. Core positions in buildings can be classified into three types: the 'centre core', the 'double core' and the 'single core'. In the tropics, the cores should preferably be located on the hot-sides of the building being the east and the west sides. It is evident that a double core has many benefits. By placing each of the two cores on the sides, they provide buffer zone as insulation to the internal floor spaces. Studies have shown that the minimum air-conditioning load results from using the double-core configuration in which the window openings run from north to south, and the cores are placed on the east and the west sides. These also applies to buildings in the temperate climatic zone.

central core

end core

side core

cores at hot sides

• The lift lobbies, stairways and toilets zone are areas that should be given natural ventilation and a view out where possible. This means that they inevitably should be placed at the periphery of the useable floor-space as against being placed in the central-core position. External periphery placements of these parts of the building result in energy savings since these areas would not require mechanical ventilation, and require reduced artificial lighting besides eliminating the need for additional mechanical pressurisation ducts for fire-protection purposes. Aesthetically, by placing these on the periphery of the building, these areas receive natural sunlight and provide views to the outside which with a central core position would not be possible. In this way the building user on leaving at the upper floor can see out and be aware of the place (instead of entering an artificially lit lobby that could be anywhere in the world.

view out from lobby

awareness of place

• Tall building are exposed more directly to the full impacts of external temperatures and radiation heat. Accordingly, the overall building's orientation has important bearing on energy conservation. In general, arranging the building with its main and broader openings facing north-south shows the greatest advantage with regard to reducing the building's solar insolation (and it's air-conditioning load). As frequently happens, the geometry of the site would not coincide with the north-south geometry of the sun. In which case, the other built-elements of the building may if expedient for planning purposes follow the geometry of the site (e.g. to optimise upon basement carparking layouts, etc.). The typical floor window openings should generally face the direction of the least direct solar insolation (i.e. north-south in the tropics). Some corner shading adjustments or shaping may need to be made for those site locations which lie further north or south of the tropics or for non-conformity of building plan to the solar path. Generally the window openings should orientate north-south unless important views require other orientations or openings. If required for aesthetic reason, curtain-wall may be used on these non-solar facing facades. On the other building faces, some for of solar shading is required while also taking into consideration the quality of light entering the spaces. In temperate zones, these transitional space can have adjustable glazing at the outer face so that the balcony or recesses can act as 'sun-spaces' to collect solar-heat positively like green-houses, conservation, sun-room, etc.

side/building adjustments

curtain wall at North & South faces

• Deep recesses may be used at the building's hot sides to give shading. A window can be totally recessed to become balconies or become small-'sky-courts' that can synergistically serve a number of other functions besides sun-shading. Placing balconies at the hot-elevations permit the glazing to these areas to be full-height clear panels. These can be

recessed sun-spaces

---

sliding openable panels to give access to these balcony spaces. The balcony spaces can serve as evacuation spaces in case of emergencies, as large terraces for planting and landscaping, as a flexible zone for the addition of future executive wash-rooms or kitchenette facilities.

• Large multi-storey transitional spaces might be introduced in the central and periphery parts of the building as air-spaces and atriums. These serve as "in-between" zones located between the insides and the outside of the building. These should be designed to function in a similar to that of the traditional 'verandahway' in the old shop-houses or of the porches in the early 19th century masonry houses in the tropics Atriums should not be totally enclosed but should be placed in this in-between space between the insides and the outsides and whose tops could be shielded by a louvred-roof to encourage wind-flow through the inner areas of the building. These may also be designed to function as wind-scoops to bring and to control natural ventilation to the inner parts of the building.

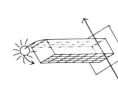

site/building/solar skycourts

transitional spaces

• The external walls of the building should be regarded more as a permeable environmentally-interactive membrane with adjustable openings (rather than as a seled-skin). In temperate climate, the external wall has of course, to serve both very cold winters as well as hot summers. In which case, the external wall should be filter-like and have variable parts that provide good insulative functioning in the cold periods and be operable in the hot seasons. Where in the tropics, the external wall should have moveable parts that control and enable good cross-ventilation for internal comfort, provide solar protection from the sun, regulate any wind-swept rain besides facilitating the rapid discharge of any heavy rain-fall.

environmentally-interactive wall

• The building plan in addition to responding to the commercial intentions of the building (e.g. enabling single, double or multiple tenancies situations) should be reflective of the pattern of life and culture of the place and climate. Partly this involves an understanding of the spatial modalities of people, the way they work, the way culture arranges privacy and community. This can be reflected in the plan's configuration, its depth, the position and configuration of the entrance and exits, the means of movement through and between spaces, the orientation and external views as interpreted in the plan, and others. At the same time, the plan should also reflect the air movements through the spaces and provision of sunlight into the building. The space for work even in a high-rise commercial structure has to have some degree of humanity, some degree of interest and some degree of scale. For instances, the use of large terraces and skycourts might serve as communal spaces as well as ventilating spaces into the upper parts of tall building.

plan/use pattern/ventilation

balconies & terraces

• The ground floor in the tropics should preferably be open to the outside and be a naturally ventilating space. The ground floor relation to the street is also important. The introduction of the internalised indoor atrium at the ground floor may mean the demise of street-life. Free-standing fortress-like buildings also tend to separate the building from the pavement and further alienate the street. By being set back, it eliminates pedestrian movement and reduces the communication and movement into and around buildings from traffic and access points. Free-standing buildings become isolated buildings on isolated plots depicting an "island site"

open-to-sky ground floor

Ken Yeang's design principles and agenda are clearly laid out independently of actual projects but are informed by them.

central issues are the development of a new regional form of architecture and the task of designing a well-tempered environmentally responsive form of architecture. Most of Ken Yeang's work is in his home town of Kuala Lumpur, where the tropical climate, combined with increasing land values and an incredible acceleration in the rate of construction, poses special problems. When writing about Ken Yeang, Dennis Sharp quotes the locally popular saying 'that more has been built in the last decade than in the whole of the previous century'. Consequently Ken Yeang's practice finds itself more often than not working for commercial developer clients to design tall buildings for tight urban sites. The problem, for Yeang then, reduces to how to build the environmentally interactive skyscraper.

This is something about which Ken Yeang thinks a great deal, either in connection with a particular project or more theoretically. The fundamental difficulty here is that while Malaysian culture is currently undergoing a period of self-assertion there are simply no precedents for this kind of architecture. This is not unique to Malaysia but is common to all the Pacific Rim countries, and cities experiencing extensive urban growth such as Singapore, Bangkok, Jakarta, Manila, Tokyo and Hong Kong. During the early years of expansion architects tended to rely upon existing Western precedents for the design of high-rise buildings. More recently there has rightly been a reaction against this with a demand for the application of more traditional Malay forms. Ken Yeang is rather against the development of any artificial style[3] but has instead developed what he calls his 'design principles and agenda for a well-tempered architecture' which can be seen as a sort of design guide for these situations. Nearly all these issues can be seen to reflect topics about which Ken Yeang has thought more theoretically.

We can thus see here a design process which is in effect split into two distinct but related phases. The more general process of the theoretical development of the design guidelines was clearly given great impetus by Ken Yeang's early work at Cambridge, but continues to be informed by each project. However, the project design task itself is to take these principles and apply them alongside the many other problems which are special to the site, brief and client.[4]

In practice, of course, Ken Yeang argues that most architects work this way. 'Any architect with a mind of his own somehow whether by design or default will produce an architecture which is identifiable to that architect.' While this may be true, Ken Yeang has developed this articulated process to a particularly high degree of organization and clarity. This also helps to ameliorate the effects of any turnover of staff that he regrets but accepts as part of the local economic circumstances in which he has to work. New staff can read and study not just past designs but also the principles upon which they are based together with the firm's project management manual. However, these new staff may bring in and apply their own interpretation of these ideas, thus renewing the practice.

With the practice at its current size Ken Yeang must delegate a considerable amount to his staff. He thinks hard about how to manage this disparate, talented and individualistic group of designers. 'I have to be very dependent on my architects and each one of them has their own personal way of doing things and I try to respect that.' Thus he recognizes the need to adapt his style of management to suit the individual. 'It's a matter of adopting the appropriate leadership style to the job in hand and the individual in question; authoritarian, democratic, liberal, free rein.' Ken Yeang expects his architects to generate ideas within the carefully defined design process, and prefers to allow them maximum

[3]**Style**
Along with others, most notably Eva Jiricna, Richard MacCormac, and Michael Wilford, Ken Yeang does not see style as a design generator. He argues here that a new Pacific regional urban style must emerge from the process of research and synthesis on a series of similar problems, rather than be applied to that process like a straightjacket.

[4]**Guiding principles**
Some argue that the design process is a contribution to knowledge and understanding and therefore is itself an exercise in research. The recent attempts to measure the research output of university departments in the United Kingdom have been particularly difficult to operate in the design areas such as architecture. In this sense a work of design, like a work of art, may advance our appreciation, but since design also functions it may increase our technical as well as cultural knowledge. The public consumers of architecture rarely recognize that good buildings may not only solve the client's problems but may also have a research component for their designers. See also particularly the footnotes on this topic in the chapters on Herman Hertzberger and Denise Scott Brown and Robert Venturi.

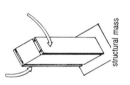

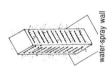

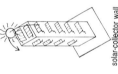

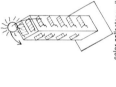

conditions.

• Planting and landscaping should be used not only for their ecological and aesthetic benefits but also as cooling devices for the buildings. Planting should be introduced as 'vertical landscaping' to the faces of the building and to the inner courts of the upper parts of the tall building. Plants absorb carbon dioxide and generate oxygen that contributes to their cooling effect benefitting the building and its surrounds.

vertical landscaping

• Solar shading is essential to all wall glazed areas facing directly the solar insolation sides (i.e. generally East and West in the tropics). A number of possible configurations in passive devices can be used (e.g. fins, spandrels, egg-crates, etc.) depending on the orientation of the building facade. Shading blocks the solar isolation in the summer and prevents heat penetration into the building being all year round in the tropics and in the summer months in temperate zone.

shading devices

• In temperate climates, the use of air-locks prevents the loss by air-leakages to make the building air-tight lowering its heat-loss and thereby conserving energy.

• Cross-ventilation should be permitted to internal spaces (even in air-conditioned spaces, to allow for occasions of system breakdowns). Air ventilation lets fresh air in and exhausts hot room air out. Good air movement promotes heat emissions from the human body surface and gives greater feeling of comfort. The use of skycourts balconies and atriums as open spaces and

wind-ducts

wind-scoops

transitional spaces at the upper parts of the skyscraper encourages wind flow into the internal spaces. We can also use side vents as 'sky wind-scoops' located at edges of the skyscraper facade to capture and optimise on the high wind-speed at the upper levels where the wind can be channelled into ceiling plenums to ventilate inner recessed spaces.

• Good thermal insulation of the building skin will reduce heat transfer through the skin, both from solar heat gain from the outside and loss of coolness from the inside to the outside. In temperate locations, insulation will reduce the heat loss from the building in winter and prevent heat penetration in summer. A second skin (i.e. a rain-wall) can be built over the inner wall with an air gap in between.

insulative walls

• Structural building mass can be used such that it stores the heat so that the mass is cooled at the night-time and keep the internal spaces cool in the day time. In temperate climates structural and building mass will absorb the solar heat in the day time to be released at night.

structural mass

• A system of water-spray to the building facade is a method to promote evaporation. Water is sprayed periodically by means of a sprinkler-system to the hot faces of the building for evaporative cooling. In the case of temperate climates, these would be used in the summer months.

water-spray wall

• In temperate climates, solar-window or the solar-collector wall can be located on the outer face of the building as a substitute for an external skin to inlet solar heat positively.

solar-collector wall

More of Ken Yeang's 'guiding principles' and a typical building to which they were applied.

freedom within this constraint. 'I don't always lead a project in terms of design form, or do the first sketch, but only if the designer finds difficulty in interpreting the client's brief or the site's planning constraints.'[5]

Ken Yeang likes to progress a project in clearly understood and defined stages. Usually when dealing with a commercial client he likes to start with an extremely short brief. 'I'm not interested in the brief so much as finding out what the client's objectives are and in most cases that should not be more than one line, a mission statement!' Once this is established the project itself is processed through a carefully controlled series of stages from inception to completion. Of these stages three are of interest here and they are what Ken Yeang chooses to call 'pre-design', 'schematic design' and 'design development'.

The 'pre-design' phase must establish the financial and physical feasibility of the project by establishing the 'return on investment or ROI' which is done in-house. At this stage Ken Yeang is careful not to get drawn into designing at all, but rather keeping to the discipline of only working out feasibility. He feels that too many architects are so keen to begin designing that they develop projects which have little or no chance of being realized.[6] Proving feasibility in this commercial climate involves little more than telling the client what can be done on the site, what the costs will be and what returns can be achieved:

A feasibility study should not take more than two pages, but in those two pages we make assumptions on building form, on the number of basements and storeys, the standard of building, roughly what we would like to do. We work out the potential of the site and include a little contingency. It is at this stage that we explore and present alternatives.[7]

Ken Yeang will repeat this part of the process 'again and again until the ROI looks good, but if the ROI cannot be made acceptable we do not proceed with schematic design at all'. This emphasis on cost control is not seen by Ken Yeang as restrictive or constraining but rather as a part of the creative design environment. He believes that only by understanding the 'objectives of the building' at this stage can sensible budgets be set within which the remaining design process can operate with some degree of freedom. 'A useful guideline is to ask early on to what extent the building exists as a symbol, as an enclosure, an a marketable product or as an investment.' Ken Yeang argues that, unless the designer shares a similar understanding about this to the client, he is likely to get involved in 'cost-cutting' later on rather than 'cost control' throughout. 'Cost control means a discriminate and controlled allocation of cost in a building so we are spending money where it matters.'[8]

Once the scheme passes this initial stage then effectively the brief has now been established and 'schematic design' can begin. It is at this point that Ken Yeang's central design process comes into operation. Here he delegates to one of his design architects.[9] This requires careful choice. 'We match the person to the job.' This job architect is given considerable freedom by Ken Yeang to work in their own way, but should investigate and extend the ideas and themes within the broad R and D guidelines which he has laid down. These principles are clearly articulated, but only in diagrammatic form, thus leaving considerable freedom to the individual designer to interpret them in each particular situation. Ken stresses that these 'should never be applied as a formula or allowed to inhibit inventive design'. The guidelines cover such matters as the number and general disposition of service cores, staircases and lifts, the orientation of the

[5]Intervention
Ken Yeang seems to agree with Michael Wilford's view of himself as an 'editor'. However, as we shall see, Ken Yeang sets a very clear agenda of design objectives for his staff so they are given freedom within a very carefully controlled format. In this sense there are close parallels between Ken Yeang and John Outram, who also has a well-documented design process.

[6]Designing too soon
Most designers seem to have such an enthusiasm for the business of designing itself that they can perhaps easily be tempted into abortive work of this nature. Design may perhaps be seen as a drug, with its addicts needing fairly regular fixes. Architects who join universities to teach after a substantial career in practice often find that they have almost no time to design when developing their academic career and describe their feelings as being like withdrawal symptoms.

[7]Alternatives
The alternatives here set out the various possible geometrical configurations such as the height and number of buildings, the shape of the floor plate, whether car parking will be in a number of basement floors or on an above-ground podium. These fundamental geometrical factors seem fairly similar to the basic planning alternatives presented at an equally early stage by Michael Wilford.

[8]Cost
This is an interesting distinction. Ken Yeang is effectively advancing the argument that cost need not be seen, as it often is, as a restriction on creativity. If the design process proceeds without his exercise in 'cost control', then the 'cost cutting' which inevitably has to be made later appears to remove much of the designer's invention. However, Ken Yeang finds that, by contrast, if appropriate cost targets are set early in the process and adhered to then the designer is given considerable freedom by the client. Robert Venturi talks of how he enjoys facing what he calls the 'reality of the budget'.

[9]Design staff
I am particularly grateful to Emmy Lim Ying-Li, Nimesh Choksi, Azahari Muhammad, Indrani Vanniasingham and Yeoh Gim Seong, who all spent time helping me to understand this interesting relationship between Ken Yeang and his design staff. The work on their drawing boards and the ideas they discussed clearly confirmed the extent to which they could use their own approach and generate their own ideas within the very clear process structure laid down by Ken Yeang. It is also interesting to note that Ken Yeang has since written to the author that 'an interesting outcome of our meeting is the clarification of our own modus operandi and it has contributed

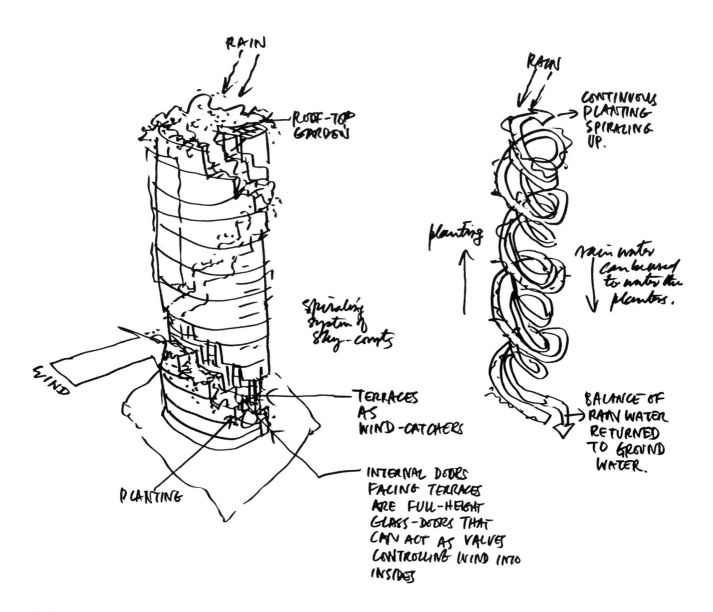

RAIN

ROOF-TOP GARDEN

WIND

spiraling system of sky-courts

PLANTING

TERRACES AS WIND-CATCHERS

INTERNAL DOORS FACING TERRACES ARE FULL-HEIGHT GLASS-DOORS THAT CAN ACT AS VALVES CONTROLLING WIND INTO INSIDES

RAIN

CONTINUOUS PLANTING SPIRALING UP.

planting

rain water can be used to water the planters.

BALANCE OF RAIN WATER RETURNED TO GROUND WATER.

Early sketches and development drawings show the way Ken Yeang applies his 'guiding principles' to a design project.

building and, most particularly, its chief glazing and shading systems, the use of recesses, balconies and other devices to introduce shading, the use of multi-storey atria at high levels within the building to generate air movement, the design of the external skin, solar shading devices, planting and landscaping, the key role of the ground floor, and the organization of the plan.

The result of this process is 'a set of quick free-hand schematic design sketches, quick because the commercial client usually wants it fast and so it is usually done in less than a week'. However, the emphasis on cost control is maintained with 'good quantity surveyor costings which must correlate with the cost targets produced earlier for the ROI'. Ken Yeang finds that provided this is ensured then 'the client usually leaves our architecture alone'. The return on investment study is now redone in detail and rough physical models and possibly 3-D computer models are built to test particular features of the design. Once all this is cleared with the client 'design development' begins, which usually involves computer-aided draughting and fully finished physical models.[10]

In spite of his academic background and research orientation Ken Yeang does not favour an overly open-ended approach to design. He does not believe in producing alternative designs at this stage and certainly would not show these to a client. 'If you think too much about the scheme you'll probably come up with two or three alternative solutions and with maybe half a dozen other options, but if you approach a scheme with a gut feeling then can only be one solution but billions of options.'[11] Ken Yeang frequently refers to Peter Cook, who has obviously made a great impact on his thinking about the design process. He shares Peter Cook's view that 'the best designers are the ones with a heightened sense of intuition'. He believes that 'you cannot teach a student to design, but you can teach him to develop his sense of intuition and design confidence'.[12] In particular, Ken Yeang believes the starting point for the design process has to be a matter of intuitive judgement:

I trust the gut feeling, the intuitive hand, the intuitive feel about the project ... you can technically solve accommodation problems, you can solve problems of view and so on but which problem to solve first is a gut feeling ... you can't explain it but you feel that's right and nine times out of ten you are right.

However, Ken Yeang is quite clear about the importance of finding what he likes to call the 'Key Factors for Success' very early in each project:

We look at each project and try to see it from the client's point of view ... and then we try to have a feel about what is the big idea, what are the key factors for success, and we do little 3-D diagrams ... and we say to each other 'look you know I think there has to be a great view down here, and maybe a column, the lift core is down here, some sort of platform that sticks out', and this is how I feel.

[10]Role of consultants

Ken Yeang believes that this approach gives the quantity surveyor a role as a design collaborator rather than casting him or her in an adversarial role with the architect. See also Herman Hertzberger's comments, which reflect a similar approach.

[11]Alternatives

This is very much in contrast to some of our other designers, including Michael Wilford and Eva Jiricna in particular, who see the generation of alternatives as a key element in their design process. Perhaps one of the factors here is that Ken Yeang appears generally to work with clients who insist on progressing the early design stages very quickly. Ken Yeang considers the presenting of alternatives as the 'designer who cannot make up his own mind and wasteful of talent and resources'. He says that 'all too often the client will choose the alternative that the designer least prefers'.

[12]Intuition

In psychological terms intuition is a rather vague concept. All too often this term is used to refer to the residue of behaviour which is left after we have explained what we can. It is certainly being used here to mean behaviour which the designer does not control deliberately or even necessarily understand. It is also, by implication, behaviour which is like a highly developed skill, in that it almost certainly draws heavily on experience. The ability to recognize situations and their many variants is a characteristic of the practitioners of highly developed cognitive skills. For example, studies of chess grandmasters have suggested that rather than analyse situations they simply recognize them. It seems probable that experienced designers similarly recognize aspects of design problems and therefore know how to respond. It may therefore be that Ken Yeang and Peter Cook here are talking about education in its most general sense, that is, having the widest possible exposure to relevant material.

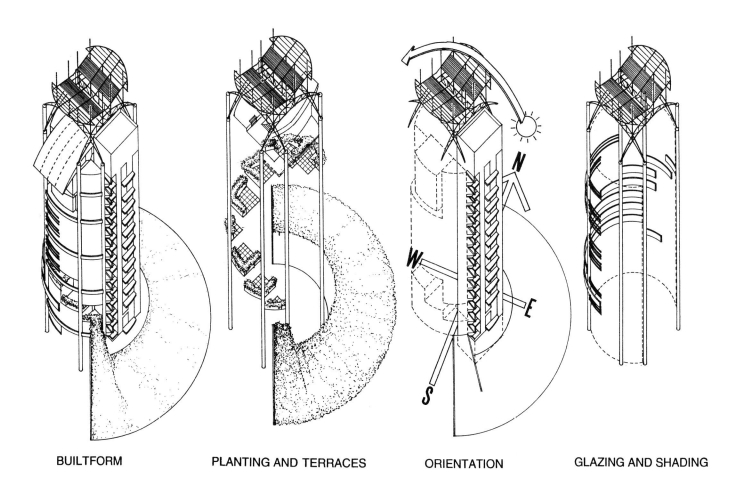

BUILTFORM   PLANTING AND TERRACES   ORIENTATION   GLAZING AND SHADING

Ken Yeang tends to draw while he talks and believes that this process is quite natural. 'It's almost impossible for an architect to think without drawing.' He feels that design ideas emerge as a result of this interaction with the drawing.[13] He has argued that the debate as to whether designers preconceive their solutions or not is pointless, but agrees with Donald Schon's view of the designer holding a conversation with his drawing. Ken Yeang has simultaneously criticized his fellow-professionals for too often designing without thinking, and for thinking too much without designing:

Thoughtfulness is not synonymous with theory. A work of architecture can be thoughtful but not necessarily theoretical. What is important is that the ideas, thinking and premises underlying the creation and design of the building should be didactic.[14]

While the practice clearly has a well-developed and finely tuned design process Ken Yeang also devotes a considerable slice of his time to marketing. This is not some cynical promotional exercise but an organized and budgeted business function based on a continual review of both the nature of the service he gives and of its marketplace. He is quite prepared to use conventional business marketing analysis techniques which require him to view his activity as 'selling a product into a market'. This, he feels, helps him to apply different marketing strategies for different design situations. 'Are you selling the same product you have been for years to the same clients or market, or are you developing a new product or trying to get new clients?' He warns designers against failing to see the problems of educating the market to accept their ideas or of trying to design without understanding the state of their market:

I was talking about marketing professional services as a crucial component of professional practice in 1976 and people thought I was crazy, they thought I was violating the code of conduct, but I said that's the way to go, you have to systematize how you get business and that's what marketing does. Marketing does not guarantee success but it gives you an orderly method of getting business, at least you know where your pitfalls are, what you have done wrong and how to improve, then you don't have everything as intuition.

This wish to systematize the process of design and its context while respecting and encouraging the intuitive skills of his designers seems to summarize Ken Yeang's attitude to his profession. He represents a designer who thinks a great deal about implementing an investigative theoretical and inventive agenda for his practice and about how to manage people so that agenda can continue to be realized. In short, he continues through design to research and develop his thinking about issues of his own choosing, he satisfies his clients and produces award-winning architecture. The fact that he achieves this with such a socially and culturally responsible agenda by working almost exclusively with highly commercial clients suggests that this process is certainly worth our attention.

[13]**Drawing**
One of our most common responses is the extent to which designers find that drawing mediates and facilitates thought. There have been references to this in many of the earlier chapters.

[14]**Research and design**
This point could share the footnote on this topic towards the beginning of this chapter.

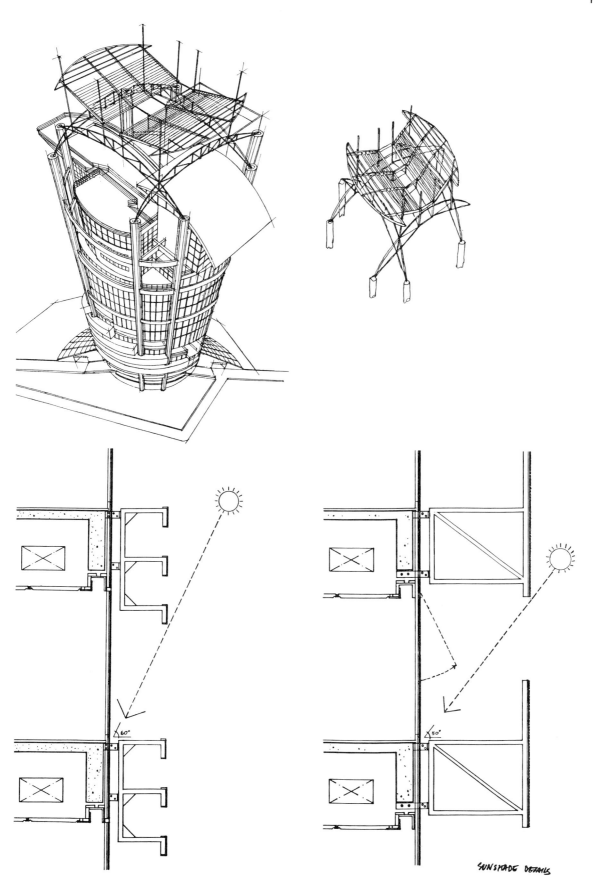

SUNSHADE DETAILS

A design drawing and details show further development of the project.

Ken Yeang
Bibliography

Morris, N. (1990). Paradigms lost in the tropics. *Architects' Journal*, 25 April, 14.

Powell, R. (1989). *Ken Yeang: Rethinking the environmental filter*, Singapore: Landmark Books.

Raman, P. G. (1990). The web of tradition: Ken Yeang's buildings in Malaysia. *Spazio Societa*, **51**, 96–105.

Sharp, D. (1989). Tropical heights. *RIBA Journal*, August, 42–56.

Sharp, D. (1989). Transformation of the traditional. *Building Design*, 3 November, 22-27.

Yeang, K. (1972). Bases for ecosystems design. *Architectural Design*, July, 434–436.

Yeang, K. (1974). The energetics of the built environment. *Architectural Design*, July, 446–451.

Yeang, K. (1978). *Tropical Urban Regionalism: building in a South-East Asian city*, Singapore: Mimar.

Yeang, K. (1987). A review of Malaysian Architecture 1957–1987. In C. C. Yoong (ed.), *Post-Merdeka Architecture* (pp. 13–29), Kuala Lumpur: Pertubuhan Akitek Malaysia.

Yeang, K. (1987). *Tropical Verandah City: Some urban design ideas for Kuala Lumpur* (second edition), Kuala Lumpur: Longmans.

Conclusions

This book has examined the work of a small number of distinguished architects and has raised interesting questions about both the variety and consistency of design practice. While the designers studied here represent a wide range of approaches and attitudes they were remarkably consistent in the issues they raised in discussion.

Many of these issues can be picked out from the running notes to be found in each chapter and reference to the main text alongside these notes will amplify this discussion. Throughout the book the notes have, where possible, been given similar titles in order to facilitate comparison. However, these titles can at times be misleading and, in reality, the whole subject is not so easily compartmentalized as the notes may suggest. For example, the size and structure of the office, the way the design team works, the relationships and communication between principal and other staff and the role of clients in the process are all inexorably intertwined. They are separated here for the purpose of analysis and discussion.

This chapter reviews a number of the key issues which were raised by a significant number of the designers.

Office size and structure

The evidence presented in this book would suggest that it is possible to run a highly successful and admired design practice with many different approaches to the organization of staff. The most obvious distinction which can be drawn is between the single named principal practices of Santiago Calatrava, Herman Hertzberger, Eva Jiricna, John Outram and Ian Ritchie and the multi-partner practices of Ahrends, Burton and Koralek, MacCormac, Jamieson and Prichard, Venturi Scott Brown, Stirling and Wilford and Hamzah and Yeang.

Not surprisingly, there tends to be less variation in the organization and structure of the single-principal practices. They are all very much dependent on the reputation of one person and thus this individual seems to take a hand in every project and consequently rarely runs one.

Ahrends, Burton and Koralek seem to operate almost as three federated practices sharing resources and some staff, but with each original named partner and his newer partner working with their own job teams. A similar structure can be found in the practice of Hamzah and Yeang. By comparison, Stirling and Wilford, until the sad and untimely death of James Stirling, operated more as a single practice with both partners involved in all jobs. Robert Venturi and Denise Scott

Brown tend to run their own jobs but both partners are involved in most projects. MacCormac, Jamieson and Prichard seem to be configured more along corporate lines with each partner playing a particular and defined role, taking responsibility for certain stages of work rather than individual projects. All these practices, however, showed some flexibility in their organization and seemed willing and able to bend to suit the conditions.

Even among the multi-partner practices there is quite a strongly held view that clients expect to deal with the titular head. Although his office is a partnership, Ken Yeang is quite outspoken in his support for this view that a corporate structure is unlikely to succeed here. Robert Venturi and Denise Scott Brown take a similar position and have developed a sophisticated model of distributed management, after previously being organized more along corporate lines.

Many of our participants made reference to the size of their practice in terms of the size they would like it to be. Of course, in reality practices are subject to the ravages of a notoriously cyclical building industry, and the sizes quoted here probably reflect these external economic pressures more than some deliberately planned target size. However, most made comments about a notional ideal size which seems to be based on a feeling about relationships and communication, confirming how important it is to see design as a group rather than an individual process. The principals of most of the single-partner practices seem to like a practice of between 15 and 25. Ian Ritchie, Herman Hertzberger and Eva Jiricna were quite explicit about this. We have already seen that Richard MacCormac's practice, operating as a single unit on a sort of corporate basis, also likes to be around two dozen or so, as does Stirling Wilford and Associates where the partners functioned almost as one. Richard Burton's practice, by contrast, operates more like three units and has up to 50 staff. Ken Yeang has a similarly constructed arrangement.

The design team

Ian Ritchie was quite explicit about the establishment of human relationships within the practice. His five groups of five can be seen as a conscious attempt to build close and thus productive relationships. The actual number in each group must, of course, vary according to the size of the particular job or project in hand, but there seems to some consensus that working in design teams of about five feels about right, allowing for a variety of ideas and yet keeping communication fairly tight.

In design terms the interaction between the principal and the project architects seems very close. The physical accommodation is often such that access to the principal is very easy and open. For example, Eva Jiricna can often be found sitting in the middle of the office with one or other of her designers, while Ian Ritchie can be seen moving around his drawing office from board to board with his sketchbook. The room in which John Outram works also contains files, computers and photocopiers, with staff coming and going almost constantly. James Stirling and Michael Wilford shared an 'open-door' office.

Herman Hertzberger has a rather more formalized channel of communication, using his beloved A3 pad. Both Herman Hertzberger and Ian Ritchie specifically mentioned the need to go home and do their own design thinking, perhaps in the evening, returning ideas to the design team the next morning.

The design team
Richard Burton 2
Santiago Calatrava 22
Herman Hertzberger 28
Richard MacCormac 54
John Outram 66
Ian Ritchie 76
Michael Wilford 98
Ken Yeang 110, 114, 116

The flow of ideas and the relationship between principal and the design team also showed variety. Michael Wilford drew a parallel between himself and a newspaper editor to explain how ideas came from his designers, while Herman Hertzberger feels that he initiates all major design concepts. Some principals, most notably John Outram and Ken Yeang, give their designers considerable freedom but only within very clear published guidelines as to how the process should proceed.

Several of the sole principals described themselves as not actually 'running' any particular job in the practice, but rather overseeing them all. This is, however, probably far too simplistic a notion to be useful without further elaboration. Such principals obviously have great demands on their time in a way probably best summed up in Ian Ritchie's words. 'The commitment we make to quality requires a very much day-in day-out relationship with clients and consultants and everybody else, and I can't do that if I am running a job.' What this seems to mean in the practices studied here is that the business of managing the progress of each job is delegated to a particular member of staff in the office. The involvement of the principal or partner waxes and wanes as the design process develops. We shall see in the next section how there are both extremely intense moments and more relaxed periods.

Intervention

It is clear that design proceeds best through very closely knit teams which also benefit from time to time from some external intervention which breaks into their smooth operation. Richard MacCormac, Richard Burton and Ken Yeang all made specific reference to the need to stop a group becoming too inward and self-reinforcing.

In the early years of their practice, Richard Burton wrote about the way the three original partners of ABK were used to intervene in the working of their design groups. Their policy then was to use one partner to run the job and deal with the client with another partner supporting him. The third, however, would not normally make any contact with the client or become involved in the running of the job, but could be used to intervene with a more detached view than might be expected from the members of the design team.

Richard MacCormac refers to his role as 'making a series of interventions at different stages of the design process'. As well as architectural judgement, this also seems to require a good sense of timing. He talks of creating a crisis by recognizing that something is not right with the scheme and then finding someone to work with in the team who understands this crisis. Michael Wilford portrays a rather less confrontational view of his interventions into the design team's working. He likens his role to that of the newspaper editor who receives copy from his journalists and suggests how it might be changed or given different emphasis.

It is clearly not possible for the principals of design practices such as those studied here to be involved with every project team on a daily basis. The way in which they interact with the design is itself therefore a matter worth our study. Robert Venturi and Denise Scott Brown, for example, describe a process not unlike that to be found in schools of design based on the 'studio and crit'. Eva Jiricna, Ian Ritchie and Ken Yeang all described their role as not actually running any particular job but keeping an eye on all of them. It is interesting to note also that all three explicitly recognized the need to intervene differently with each member of their staff. For example, Eva Jiricna described how she would see some staff several times a day while others would only be seen once a week.

A common feature, then, which connects many of the designers in this book is the way in which they combine a degree of detachment with skilfully timed interventions into the working of the design team.

Sense of purpose

The strong sense of purpose that designers feel was one of the characteristics most commonly discussed and perhaps enables the practice principal to make disruptive interventions into the working of the design team without collapsing the whole process. Other studies have shown that a commitment to the ideas behind their designs is one of the things that architects value most highly. Many of our architects feel that practising architecture is a highly stressful business, and that without this deep underlying sense of purpose it would not a be a viable way of earning a living. It is perhaps not surprising that these feelings were most strongly expressed by the single-partner principals who not only have their name personally attached to output of the practice but also bear the ultimate responsibility for the business. Ken Yeang, Eva Jiricna, Ian Ritchie and Richard MacCormac all made similar points about this.

A strongly shared sense of purpose, once achieved, seems to bind design teams together. However, students who are forced together into design groups at university tend to find this difficult to develop quickly. Designers are often original and open in their thinking and do not naturally form shared understandings of this kind. It is perhaps therefore one of the most precious attributes of the successful design team. Perhaps in the end, architects and other designers work long and unsociable hours not for financial reward and probably not out of a sense of duty to their client but rather out of dedication to the ideals they share. Richard MacCormac in particular pointed out that the difficulties and obstacles in the way of getting a design idea realized as a building are so great that it simply will not happen without this dedicated sense of purpose.

Sense of purpose
Richard MacCormac 56
Ian Ritchie 78

The brief

Richard MacCormac believes that sometimes the real problem is actually concealed by the way a brief is written. It seems that there is often a misunderstanding by clients of the kind of document designers actually want. Certainly, the kind of brief designers get is extremely variable in size and comprehensiveness. For architects, at one end of the spectrum, we might get a site owned by the client and accessible and we might even get a complete schedule of all the spaces required, including their sizes, their functions, and relationships with other spaces. At the other end of the spectrum the client may have a site and be wondering what to do with it, or may want a building and have no site. The client may have little or no idea of their needs or budget and so on. It is therefore quite commonly the case that the brief contains only a tiny fraction of the total information

The brief
Herman Hertzberger 28
Eva Jiricna 42
Richard MacCormac 54
Michael Wilford 98
Ken Yeang 110

needed to describe the problem. Eva Jiricna sums this up by saying 'we never, ever get a brief from a client which we can start working on'.

At first sight this lack of information may seem to be rather unfortunate and to present the designer with considerable difficulties. However, several of the designers in this book were clearly quite enthusiastic about working in such a situation. Herman Hertzberger, Michael Wilford and Ken Yeang all like to be given very simple and concise briefs of the kind which could be written on only one or two sheets of A4 paper. Ken Yeang even talks of a 'mission statement' which could be just several lines!

What seems to be the case here is that these designers are recognizing that the design process involves finding as well as solving problems, and they prefer to be in at the beginning and help develop the brief with the client. In working out this brief with the client, Eva Jiricna describes how 'I try to express in words what they want, and then I try to twist it into a different statement and then draw it'.

The client

Inseparably linked to the previous topic is the role of the client in the design process. Richard Burton talked of the briefing process as 'very much a matter of to-ing and fro-ing'. Michael Wilford talked of 'gradually embellishing' the brief with more detail with the client as the process develops. Richard Burton actually involved the client in the early phases of design of St Mary's Hospital and generally believes in getting the client to 'see the drawings and contribute ideas'. Robert Venturi and Denise Scott Brown talk of collaborating with their clients rather than working for them. Michael Wilford shows the client several basic alternatives in order to further develop the brief and to get the client involved and 'owning' the solution as it develops. John Outram also talks of how presenting three alternatives 'winkled out of the client what he was looking for'. Clearly there is a strong sense here that these designers prefer to have a continuing involvement of the client throughout the process. Eva Jiricna feels that 'the worst client is the person who tells you to get on with it and give me the final product'.

The word 'client' can perhaps be distinguished from the word 'customer' by an implication that the former may expect a degree of professional care not necessarily offered to the latter. Several of the designers in this book made reference to the need to establish a trusting relationship with the client. Herman Hertzberger feels that the design process cannot really succeed without this trust. His analogy with catering rather nicely suggests that we need to trust someone before we will eat a dish we have never seen before. Herman Hertzberger even tells us that he likes to watch his clients look at his drawings for the first time so that he can sense their reaction. Both Hertzberger and Ian Ritchie feel that unless they can establish and maintain a good relationship with the client the project is better abandoned. Robert Venturi and Denise Scott Brown talk of the need for the client to 'let the architect be on their side'.

One way of establishing this trust is through explanation of the process. Eva Jiricna and Herman Hertzberger, for example, made reference not only to keeping the client informed but also to educating the client about the issues under consideration. The author was struck time and time again when talking to the designers studied in this book by the amount of attention they give to communicating with the client. Just as briefs and designers vary enormously, so do clients. In this book we have discussed projects which are commissioned by individuals and others on behalf of institutions by committees. We saw how it is quite likely that in the case of large projects the client committee membership may change throughout the project, perhaps by the end even leaving the architect as the only original member of the group. The possible consequential loss of continuity and personal commitment were identified as real dangers to the design process. The extent to which the client is committed to the project is clearly thought to be critical to the success of the process. Michael Wilford believes that 'behind every distinctive building is an equally distinctive client'.

If the role of the client is so important to a successful design process this poses some serious questions about the idea of design competitions, where by the very rules of the situation, contact between designer and client is severely restricted and regulated. Richard MacCormac describes competitions as 'rather hit and miss' because of this lack of contact. He feels that often the 'winning scheme is the one that tells the client something that they never knew before . . . something that is terribly important to them and was not in the brief'. This perhaps suggests that competitions may be good ways of getting ideas from designers but that the client may well be advised to let the eventual winner start again in a more conventional relationship.

Design problems

If the brief is not a full description of the design problem then this suggests that design involves finding and identifying problems as much as solving them. Eva Jiricna describes this as a matter of questions and answers, and thinks that learning to ask the right questions is perhaps harder than getting the answers. 'It's only a matter of time to find the answers, but the question is the difficult part.'

The extent to which problem finding and problem solving are integrated into the design process remains one of the central questions of design research. Herman Hertzberger feels they can and should be more separated than some have suggested, and uses a football analogy to describe his position. 'Sometimes you are in a position where you must direct it [the ball] with one touch, but most of the time when you are not under stress you first stop the ball.' On the other hand, Richard MacCormac tells us that 'issues which are the stuff of the thing often only come out when you try to solve [problems]'.

There is much evidence in this book about the crucial need to maintain a sense of balance throughout the design process. Richard Burton talked of 'the twenty or so major issues a designer of buildings has to consider'. There are many references to the balance between artistic and technical problems. Ian Ritchie's amusing image of the poetic and technical parrots sitting on his shoulders show a deep underlying concern to balance this content of his work. As Richard Burton says, 'it's about putting it all together'.

Most of the designers in this book see technological problems as of secondary importance or even as tertiary considerations, as Michael Wilford puts it. Santiago Calatrava makes a particularly interesting point when he tells us that technical innovation more often arises out of solving problems in a particular design situation rather than thinking about the technology in a purely abstract way. Robert Venturi believes that building design should generally be technologically conservative.

Abstraction and reality

Is design always design even when practised without a client and for purely theoretical reasons? Today there is much 'paper architecture' and there are even several quite well-known architects who have actually built very little. Some of the designers in this book made specific reference to their need to design in what they called 'real' situations. Santiago Calatrava and Robert Venturi, in particular, emphasized this distinction between design in the abstract and in a real context. Santiago Calatrava seemed to imply that he thought that he had grown out of designing in the abstract and was no longer as interested as he would have been earlier in his career to design 'a pillar or an arch', but rather now feels 'you need a very precise problem and you need a place'. Robert Venturi talks of how he 'loves to face reasonably nasty reality'.

These comments imply, to a degree, an enjoyment of problem solving, perhaps akin to that we get when doing puzzles. There is a suggestion here that designers have minds which need an externally imposed problem in order to be stimulated to perform their best work. There are considerable difficulties over drawing a boundary between what we call art and what we call design, but this evidence is perhaps helpful here. At one extreme is the artist who wishes nothing more than to be left alone to express ideas through a chosen medium, setting and exploring entirely self-generated problems. Most designers like to have some of that freedom but also seem to enjoy what Venturi calls 'reasonably nasty reality'.

There is another interesting question here about the way knowledge is advanced through art and design. Santiago Calatrava clearly believes that technical innovation is more likely to result from the solving of real rather than abstract problems, and the history of inventions and engineering breakthroughs would certainly support this argument. There is a curious paradox here when this principle is applied to architecture and civil engineering. It is often the unique features of a site which make a building or structure special, thus requiring the designer to take a novel approach. However, the result may then become part of the accepted orthodoxy and get copied and reworked by other designers. It is an interesting question as to whether Frank Lloyd Wright would ever have developed the particular forms we see at Falling Water without the very special features of that site.

Guiding principles and primary generators

It must be clear from the chapters in this book that designers bring their own intellectual programme with them into each project. In some cases this programme is the result of a lifetime of study and development and has been laid out in books, articles or lectures. Perhaps the most notable examples among the designers in this book would include Herman Hertzberger's well-known publications on 'structuralism' (Hertzberger, 1971, 1991), Robert Venturi and Denise Scott Brown's work on 'Postmodern' urbanism (Venturi, 1977; Venturi, et al., 1977), and Ken Yeang's books on regionalism and ecology in the tropics (Yeang, 1978). In other cases critics have analysed the work of designers and developed the argument for them. In recent years there have been major books written about the work of Ahrends, Burton and Koralek (Ahrends *et al*, 1991), Santiago Calatrava (Harbison, 1992; Sharp, 1992), Eva Jiricna (Pawley, 1990) and Stirling and Wilford (Stirling & Wilford, 1984, 1990). Richard MacCormac, John Outram and Ian Ritchie are particularly prolific authors and lecturers about their approach to architecture, and many of the designers studied here hold academic posts in addition to their practice.

The books and articles referred to are the appropriate place to explore the ideas of these architects while here we must concentrate on their process rather than philosophy. However, what seems to bind all the designers together in this book is their urge to continue to learn about and develop these ideas through their design work. There is clearly a two-way process in operation here. On the one hand, each design project allows the designer to explore and develop their own intellectual programme, and in this sense the design process can itself be seen as a form of research. Herman Hertzberger is surely telling us this when he describes his Centraal Beheer office building as an 'hypothesis'.

On the other hand, this programme also provides a series of 'guiding principles' which inform each project. It is not difficult to see Santiago Calatrava's fascination for 'dynamically balanced' structures coming through in his bridges and railway stations or Michael Wilford's concern for the urban design of the public domain informing his museums, art galleries and university buildings. It is quite clear, then, that such 'guiding principles' play a highly influential role in the design process. It is from these that many of the concepts in a design flow in the form of 'primary generators' which serve to bring order and form to the early phases of the design process.

These early ideas can take many forms, and we have seen in this book how they may range from a palette of materials in Eva Jiricna's case to the site, context and basic layout in Michael Wilford's case. These 'primary generators' are not by any means fully developed designs, and perhaps are the result of studying only a few aspects of the problem. What they offer the designer is a working hypothesis, or a way of saying 'what if?' They allow for some aspects of the design to be temporarily fixed in order to study their implications, explore their consequences and develop a greater understanding of the interrelatedness of the problem as a whole.

Robert Venturi and Denise Scott Brown were careful to explain that they do not design in order to prove their theories, and indeed sometimes only begin to formulate their ideas after seeing them emerge in a number of projects. What remains clear is the value of such 'guiding principles' and 'primary generators' without which design thought would be unstructured and directionless. The evidence in this book supports the idea that designers tend to learn about their problems through attempts to solve them rather than through abstract study and analysis.

Alternatives

Our designers showed considerable variation in their attitude to the generation of alternative design solutions. We find that Eva Jiricna really explores the problem by generating alternatives in large numbers quite early in the process, eliminating them as she understands the problem better and can criticize them more fully. Michael Wilford believes in developing a small number of alternatives to show the client. John Outram has even been known to invite all his staff to generate a scheme for a project and present these almost in competition to the client. Richard Burton's description of the design process used for his St Mary's Hospital actually included client representatives in an extremely intense exercise which generated three basic alternative layouts. Both Michael Wilford and Richard Burton were working for large institutional clients and both feel that involving the client in choosing between alternatives leads to a feeling of ownership on the client's part which is helpful later when difficulties arise during the design process.

By comparison, Santiago Calatrava and Richard MacCormac are not enthusiastic about the deliberate generation of alternatives as an essential part of the design process. Ken Yeang talks of exploring very basic alternatives at the feasibility stage but is then quite strongly against the idea of trying to develop alternative schemes. His subtle distinction between solutions and options here suggests that he strongly believes in developing one underlying idea for the scheme which may be capable of generating a large number of variants.

Denise Scott Brown makes an interesting suggestion that she and Robert Venturi tend to generate more alternatives when doing town planning rather than architecture. They explain this as being due to the democratic nature of the process and complexity of problems. However Eva Jiricna, who works largely on interior design, is one of the greatest, enthusiasts for the generation of alternatives. Perhaps, then, we may conclude that the extent to which designers generate alternatives is as much to do with their own cognitive style as it is the result of the context in which they work.

The central idea

Good designs often seem to have only a very few major dominating ideas which structure the scheme and around which other relatively minor considerations are organized. Sometimes they can even be reduced to one idea known to designers by many names but most often called the 'concept' or the 'parti'. Such 'central ideas' inevitably emerge from early explorations through 'primary generators'. However, it is interesting to note how little some of these ideas may be understood until later in the process. Richard MacCormac's descriptions of the development of the designs for his Cable and Wireless College and Chapel for Fitzwilliam College as well as Ian Ritchie's descriptions of his work at La Villette are excellent illustrations of this. This is also reflected in Robert Venturi and Denise Scott Brown's neat aphorism that 'sometimes the detail wags the dog'.

The importance of this 'central idea' is not, of course, restricted to the design process. A. N. Whitehead in his presidential address to the Mathematical Association puts it rather succinctly:

The art of reasoning consists in getting hold of the subject at the right end, of seizing the few general ideas that illuminate the whole, and of persistently organizing all subsidiary facts around them. Nobody can be a good reasoner unless by constant practice he has realized the importance of getting hold of the big ideas and hanging onto them like grim death.

The need to 'hang onto the big idea like grim death' seems a particularly accurate description of the problem facing the architect. Santiago Calatrava spoke of the need to 'support the great idea right through to the end'. Richard MacCormac was quite clear about this referring to the 'big idea' keeping designers going throughout what he recognizes as a very fraught process:

This is not a sensible way of earning a living, it's completely insane, there has to be this big thing that you're confident you're going to find, you don't know what it is you're looking for and you hang on.

A similar view was expressed by Ian Ritchie, who spoke of the quality of the idea as being the 'sustenance' which 'nourishes and keeps you'. Richard MacCormac and Santiago Calatrava also both spoke of the need to share a communal understanding of this big idea which he sees as some sort of distant light that he works towards. Calatrava was insistent that the purpose of many of his drawings were ways of 'communicating to others so that they may . . . realize the idea'. Santiago Calatrava has created many sculptures as a way of expressing these central notions and Robert Venturi returns to collage even quite late in the process to ensure that the 'feeling of the "idea" is not lost'.

Parallel lines of thought

One of the characteristics of good designers seems to be their ability to develop and sustain what we might call 'parallel lines of thought'. These are arguments about some aspect of the design which may become quite sophisticated and well developed in their own right while possibly remaining unresolved with other similar notions. Eva Jiricna speaks of working on detail junctions of materials and on general spatial concepts at the same time as 'parallel processes'. Ian Ritchie's image of the two parrots of art and technology sitting on his shoulders but who from time to time jump down onto the paper suggests a similarly parallel set of processes.

A good example of parallel processes can be found in Robert Venturi's description of the development of the design for the Sainsbury Wing of the National Gallery in London's Trafalgar Square. It is clear that some ideas emerged about the way the public would access the building and how it would relate to the circulation system in the existing Wilkins Building. At another level ideas were also being developed about how the facade would work in relation to the extremely sensitive and critical urban design problems posed by such an important site. It is clear from Robert Venturi's description that these two sets of ideas became central to his thinking before being resolved into a single solution.

The problem for the designer is when the attempt should be made to reconcile all the ideas, or lines of thought, which are developing. If this is attempted too early, ideas which are still poorly understood may get lost, while if this is left too late they may become fossilized and too rigid. There is no formula or easy answer to this conundrum, the resolution of which probably depends almost entirely on the skill and sensitivity of the designer. However, what seems clear is that a degree of bravery is required to allow these lines of thought to remain parallel rather longer than might seem reasonable to the inexperienced designer.

Speed of working

Many designers have referred to the speed and intensity with which they work. The French designer and architect, Philippe Starck, has a reputation for working extraordinarily quickly. He claims that while travelling by plane on one occasion he designed a chair during the period the seatbelt signs were on for take-off. He describes this working at this speed allows him to 'capture the violence of the idea'. It is commonly held that creative work is characterized by periods of intense activity interspersed with times of quieter, more reflective contemplation. On the whole, this is confirmed by our studies here. Several specifically described the periods of intense activity as being like juggling. Richard Burton, Richard Mac-Cormac and Michael Wilford all spoke of the need to oscillate very quickly between the many issues with which an architect must be concerned. It seems that to take your mental eye off any one of these results is the equivalent of dropping a ball. Such concentration is, by nature, extremely intense and difficult to maintain for long periods. As Richard MacCormac put it, 'one couldn't juggle slowly over a long period'. Several of our designers involved in education also noted how this was one of the skills students find most difficult to acquire. Schools of design tend to use short competitions and sketch designs as ways of introducing short, intense working periods. Michael Wilford also made reference to the 'skill of prioritizing the stages at which certain inputs are valuable as distinct from an impediment to the process'. Clearly, then, it is not just the skill to juggle which is needed but also the judgement of which set of balls to pick up and when!

Several designers mentioned the need to contrast the intensity of working in the group within the office with quieter periods of solitary contemplation. Ian Ritchie and Herman Hertzberger both spoke of the need to work at home in the evening or even the early hours of the morning. The need for longer periods of quiet reflection as well as the intense periods explains why the design process cannot be hurried and compressed without considerable loss of quality. The recent idea that designers, like architects, should tender their fees competitively for this stage of the process is thus extremely dangerous. There is certainly no evidence to support the idea that the quickest and cheapest design process will give rise to the most desirable result. Indeed, bearing in mind the small part of the total cost of a building which goes on the design process, this is probably an entirely fallacious and counter-productive notion!

Drawing

The act of drawing seems particularly important to many of our designers. One of the most common observations among designers is that they actually find it hard to think without a pencil in their hand. This was mentioned by Richard MacCormac, who sees the 'pencil to be my spokesman'. Several of the designers in this book scribbled while talking to the author. In many cases their drawings contributed relatively little to the meaning simultaneously conveyed verbally, and in most cases the drawings made almost no sense at all when viewed out of the context of the conversation. However, the act of making marks on paper seems to have mediated the flow of thoughts and words. Donald Schon has referred to the architect as 'having a conversation with his drawing' (Schon, 1983) and this certainly seems to be borne out here. This seems to be what Denise Scott Brown means by the 'eye re-interpreting what the hand has done'. The drawings which designers make while thinking are frequently diagrammatic in the sense that they are not attempting to indicate three- or even two-dimensional form. Even organizing the brief is a graphically aided activity for Herman Hertzberger, and Michael Wilford likes to see the site and accommodation all drawn out to scale on quite small sheets of paper.

Frequently, drawings are overlaid and mixed together. Two-dimensional plans or sections can be seen with sketches and more diagrammatic marks all on the same piece of paper in what appears a confusing jumble. Perhaps this also reflects the intense periods of rapid alternation or juggling of issues referred to in the previous section. Michael Wilford made reference to the 'immediate process of drawing lines on paper and tracing through', and Santiago Calatrava spoke of exploring 'layer after layer . . . it is very much a dialogue'. Richard MacCormac talked of his 'thinking pencil'.

We must take very seriously this question of the need to draw in order to think, and perhaps conclude that a failure to draw may indicate a gap in thought. Certainly we have empirical evidence (Eastman, 1970) that the types of drawings done by designers correlate with the problems they both find and solve.

Herman Hertzberger, Richard Burton and Robert Venturi were all very careful to point out the difference between these 'thinking' drawings and art. Santiago Calatrava insisted that his beautiful drawings should be seen as part of a communication process with the design team rather than as works of art. The danger here is that designers become seduced by their own drawing to the point of designing it rather than the object it represents. This is a trap easily recognized by those who teach students. Ian Ritchie and Herman Hertzberger were both very conscious of the trap and careful to avoid it. However, Richard Burton also points out that his need to make good drawings is a force for clarification of ideas. Richard MacCormac referred to his 'thinking pencil' in a way which suggests that for many of these designers the pencil is almost part of them, so close and natural is the relationship.

Richard MacCormac also made explicit reference to the role of the drawing tool as a way of mediating an appropriate cognitive phase. 'These different frames of mind involve different instruments for producing and representing what you are doing.' This suggests that somehow the feel of the instrument in the hand and the way it interacts with the paper induces the right mental set. Santiago Calatrava sits working with both pencils and paint brushes, and John Outram has a box of pens and crayons open on his desk. Clearly Santiago Calatrava's close working relationship with his model maker allows him to resolve and critically evaluate through precisely engineered three-dimensional models which counteract the free-flowing water-colours which he uses to generate and suggest. Robert Venturi will sit at a computer screen in an evaluative frame of mind, and return to a collage to obtain a freer flowing statement. Marshall McLuhan taught us that the 'medium is the message', but for designers it seems that the medium is the frame of mind. No wonder that Michael Wilford speaks of the value of 'the immediate process of drawing lines on paper'.

We have already noted in an earlier section of this chapter how many of the designers here like to work on small-sized paper when designing. Eva

Jiricna, Ian Ritchie and John Outram all carried quite small pocket-sized pads around with them to sketch in. In particular Santiago Calatrava, Herman Hertzberger and Michael Wilford all referred quite specifically to their preference for using A3 paper, which they consider allows them to see the whole of the drawing at once in their line of vision.

Perhaps surprisingly, many of these highly admired and experienced designers here are quite humble about their ability to imagine three-dimensional form and space without drawing. This may be contrasted with the often-heard student excuse that although they have not yet drawn it they know how their design will look!

Computer-aided design

Several of the comments made by the designers in this book pose real problems for the developers of computer-aided design systems. Many practices seem to use the computer as a drawing and presentation tool rather than as part of the design process. Perhaps the most enthusiastic exponents of computer-aided design in this book are Ian Ritchie and Robert Venturi and Denise Scott Brown, but John Outram and Ken Yeang also make considerable use of the computer as a design tool. While these designers were quite happy to use the computer as a tool, all saw it as just another technique equivalent to, for example, drawing and physical model making. However, several designers seemed quite unhappy about integrating the computer into their design process.

There is no shortage of things computers can do which undeniably form important parts of the architectural design process. Computers can visualize three-dimensional form, they can model energy flow, they can calculate structural forces and design structural members, they can model the effects of both artificial lighting and natural light whether in the form of sunlight or daylight, they can be used as cost-estimating tools, they can offer expert advice on a whole range of technical and legislative matters, and they can even plan, albeit in a limited way. In fact they can probably do most of these things more reliably and in less time than most architects. Why, then, are so many of the architects in this book so un-enthusiastic about computers as design tools?

Their concern, as expressed here, seems to relate specifically to the issues discussed in the previous section about drawing. Michael Wilford summed up this feeling, expressing puzzlement at why designers would want to detach themselves from the immediacy of the manual drawing process. Santiago Calatrava, Richard Burton and Herman Hertzberger offered similar thoughts. Both Calatrava and Burton actually use computers in their offices, either for drafting or engineering calculations, and both were enthusiastic about the benefits of such systems. This negative view of computer-aided design, then, cannot sensibly be dismissed as an ill-informed view of the potential of computers, but rather should be taken as a serious criticism of the computer as a design partner.

Style

This section has deliberately been left to the very end. The question of style seems often to come to the forefront of the current debate about architecture and much architectural criticism seems based on attempts to define architectural 'styles' or 'movements'. However, this simply does not appear to be an issue for many of the designers studied in this book. Several of them have objected to their work being published in special issues of journals focusing on 'Post-modernism', or 'high-tech' architecture. Rather, they see these ideas as inventions of critics rather than real movements to which they subscribe. The designers studied in this book showed little or no interest in and did not perceive styles or movements as forces within their design process. Robert Venturi's comment that 'Bernini did not know he was Baroque' is a nice way of expressing this. Of course, we have studied the leaders of the field here and it may be that lesser designers pick up the more superficial aspects of contemporary practice as described by commentators and reinforce their taxonomies through imitation.

What is beyond doubt is that each of the designers discussed here have strong programmes of their own which they explore and develop through their design work. In this sense it seems reasonable to consider design to be a search after knowledge every bit as important and valuable as either art or science. A completed design has the potential to add to our pool of knowledge just as can a painting or an academic paper. Clients thus not only commission working design solutions but also support ongoing research programmes. Throughout the ages enlightened clients have understood this and have worked with their designers to the benefit not only of client and designer but also society at large. When the end product of the design process is the environment in which we live this becomes a considerable responsibility.

Bibliography

Ahrends, P., Burton, R., and Koralek, P. (1991). *Ahrends, Burton and Koralek*, London: Academy Editions.

Eastman, C. M. (1970). On the analysis of the intuitive design process. In G. T. Moore (ed.), *Emerging Methods in Environmental Design and Planning*, Cambridge, Mass.: MIT Press.

Harbison, R. (1992). *Creatures from the Mind of the Engineer: the architecture of Santiago Calatrava*, Zurich: Artemis.

Hertzberger, H. (1971). Looking for the beach under the pavement. *RIBA Journal*, **78**(8).

Hertzberger, H. (1991). *Lessons for Students in Architecture* (Ina Rike, translator). Rotterdam: Uitgeverij 010.

Pawley, M. (1990). *Eva Jiricna: Design in Exile*, London: Fourth Estate.

Schon, D. A. (1983). *The Reflective Practitioner: How professionals think in action*, London: Temple Smith.

Sharp, D. (ed.). (1992). *Santiago Calatrava*, London: Book Art.

Stirling, J., and Wilford, M. (1984). *James Stirling, Buildings and Projects*, New York: Rizzoli.

Stirling, J., and Wilford, M. (1990). James Stirling, Michael Wilford and Associates: An architectural design profile. *Architectural Design*, **60**(5–6), complete special issue.

Venturi, R. (1977). *Complexity and Contradiction in Architecture*, New York: The Museum of Modern Art.

Venturi, R., Scott Brown, D., and Izenour, S. (1977). *Learning from Las Vegas: the forgotten symbolism of architectural form*, Cambridge, Mass.: MIT Press.

Yeang, K. (1978). *Tropical Urban Regionalism: building in a South-East Asian City*, Singapore: Mimar.

Epilogue

Finally, it seems appropriate to pose a question which this book does not set out to answer but which is at least worth asking. Are there indeed some distinguishing characteristics of successful and admired designers such as those studied here? There is little doubt that all them have an abundance of what we would loosely call talent. However, there is much more to it than that. They all seem to have extraordinarily inquisitive minds which lead them into an endless search for knowledge and understanding which they enjoy pursuing through a process of solving other people's problems. This further seems to lead them to be prepared to spend a great deal of time and expend considerable effort in working with their clients. This is not only in terms of understanding what their clients think they want but also in developing an understanding in their clients of what they might be able to have.

The evidence presented here strongly suggests that design is a painful and frustrating, but ultimately extremely satisfying process involving huge intellectual commitment on the part of the designer. It also flourishes best when there is an equal commitment from the client and clearly benefits from a close and trusting relationship between client and designer. It is a process which needs slow and relaxed times as well as periods of intense activity, and which probably cannot be compressed without a loss of quality.

There are forces at work in society today which seek to reduce all things to the marketplace in which the cheapest objects and services are assumed to offer the best value. This book gives little indication to support the view that the cheapest and quickest design process is necessarily the best. One simple message has struck the author time and again during the preparation of this book, and that is the extremely demanding standards set by the designers themselves. They are quite prepared to go back over their work, even right at the last hour in order to improve and refine. They and their staff will work all night to complete a project, not because the client complained about the service provided, but simply because they are not yet content with their own work. Doctors will, of course, readily sacrifice their sleep when the patient needs emergency care, but architects, it seems, care enough to create their own crisis! To reduce such a service to competitive fee tendering seems the ultimate act of vandalism on the human intellect.

Several of the participants in this book have likened the design process to a journey through previously unexplored territory. This is in many ways a good analogy. You know roughly where you want to end up but not how to get there or what you will meet on the way, and there is even a whiff of danger about the whole enterprise. As seasoned travellers will

Design as a journey
Santiago Calatrava 18, 22
Richard MacCormac 60

know, many things can go wrong on journeys. Sir Philip Dowson warns us that 'late night euphoria, followed by a cold dawn, is a part of the journey'(Dowson and MacCormac, 1990). The relief of arriving is, of course, welcome and much anticipated, but most designers probably would agree with Robert Louis Stephenson's famous assertion that 'to travel hopefully is a better thing than to arrive, and the true success is to labour'. The author also feels the same way about this book. It has certainly not arrived at a complete or comprehensive model of the design process, and indeed it is doubtful if such a thing is really possible, but searching for it represents a fascinating journey of exploration through some of the most creative and productive minds alive today.

Dowson, P., and MacCormac, R. (1990). How architects design: design delegation. *Architects' Journal*, **192**(25-26), 28–41.